MORE LIFE AS A DOG

L.A. DAVENPORT

P-WAVE
PRESS

Copyright © 2023 by L.A. Davenport

All rights reserved.

No part of this book may be reproduced in any form or by any electronic or mechanical means, including information storage and retrieval systems, without written permission from the author, except for the use of brief quotations in a book review.

Illustrations Copyright © 2023 by L.A. Davenport.

PART I
IT'S MY PARTY

CHAPTER 1

I SINK INTO THE DEEP YET ODDLY HARD SOFA. A SOFT cloud of dust rises almost imperceptibly into the shaft of sunlight crawling its way across the room. This part of the large rambling country cottage is clearly not used very often, certainly not on a day-to-day basis. It seems reserved for special occasions. I surmise that this, my first visit since I began stepping out with the elder daughter of the household, qualifies.

That Kevin is with me only adds to the sense of occasion. Given the family are all dog lovers, I suspect they are more excited about meeting him than they are me. Naturally they have a dog of their own, a sheepdog in his venerable later years, and they have naturally assumed it would be delightful for all present if the two should meet. After all, their dog is gentle of spirit and timid by nature, until he has a ball and an opportunity to run.

His owners, like so many dog lovers I have met, are sure Kevin will adore their pet. They have doubtless heard reports that my canine companion is cute, sensitive, demonstrative, kind and somewhat delicate, as well as a fraction the size of their fine specimen. How can he not get on well with their charmer? If not like a house on fire, then certainly in an amiable and agreeable manner.

For my part, I am not sure what to do with Kevin. I have him on the sofa next to me. His head is in my lap, his body is pressed closely to my thigh. His eyes dart from person to person. As he isn't moving his head, this gives him a slightly nervous yet utterly adorable look. Add in the matching movement of his eyebrows and there is a faint air of ridiculousness about him.

Utterly adorable he may look to the outside world, but I know him much better than that. I can sense he is agitated, most likely because he can smell another dog in the house. We came across the sheepdog briefly when we arrived. He was lying on the cold tiles by the front door. I am told this is his favourite place in hot weather. I was carrying Kevin, as I often do when I enter a new and potentially confined domestic space. Consequently he didn't have time to register the presence of the other dog, let alone do anything about it. It all happened so fast, and he quickly calmed down.

Maybe he thinks the dog doesn't live here and is a visitor, like him.

I hope everything will turn out well, but I have my hand on Kevin and my fingers through his collar just in case, albeit as lightly as possible. I am trying not to transmit any sense of tension. I glance down. He looks up at me with a searching expression, a touch of worry in his huge, dark eyes. I smile casually back. He rearranges his head on my lap, but cannot re-find his previous comfortable position.

He is definitely agitated.

And I am no less worked up. I do not enjoy awkward social events. I especially don't like the getting-to-know-the-parents part of being in a relationship. In some ways, I find the parent–boyfriend axis irrelevant: my partner and I are two adults choosing to be in a relationship and we don't need anyone's approval. Yet in reality, life isn't so clean cut. For every one of us who thinks of ourselves as an adult, there are traces, sometimes stains, left over from our childhoods. Indeed, a certain part of us remains a child, our parents' child, and that part always wants their approval.

For a man in a heterosexual relationship, there is the additional complication of having to meet up to the parents' wishes for their little girl. With the father specifically, there is also a certain delicacy to be observed. None of this helps when we shake hands for the first time and I try to judge how to pitch myself to cause least offence, while demonstrating I have some spark about me.

I'm pondering this paradox while gazing down at Kevin, now apparently content, and stroking his ear. Remembering where I am, I look up and smile. They smile in return. But no one is speaking and no one seems comfortable, least of all me. So I go back to contemplating Kevin.

I amuse myself with the darting brown smudges of his eyebrows. Then I examine his grey-flecked black fur. I muse on his advancing years and how long we have been together. That and all the other-halves he has met.

I remember when an acquaintance admitted, in front of his then-girlfriend, that he had not introduced her to his grandmother because she had met too many partners and had her hopes raised too many times. And he certainly didn't want to disappoint her once again. I laugh inwardly at the recollection of his girlfriend's expression as he finished the sentence, then shudder at the number of partners Kevin has met since my divorce. How many times has he had his hopes of having a new friend raised, only to be disappointed once more? Too many.

Will this be the last new girlfriend he meets? Will this be the last awkward family introduction he has to endure?

I hope so, for both our sakes.

Still unable to face the silence all around me, I move on to the spotless-as-new floral pattern on the sofa. I wonder if it would be possible to count on the fingers of one hand the number of times any of the chairs in the room have been sat on since they arrived in the house.

What about all those fine eyelash-like hairs Kevin will undoubtedly leave behind on its pristine surface? Oh, and I didn't get a chance to wash him before we came over. Not only is he not at his shiny, sleek best, but also his belly, so comfortably supported by the sofa cushions, will be dusty after several days of long walks in the park. And there are his dirty paws to consider, too.

Then something dawns on me. My blood runs cold.

I hope Kevin doesn't get so nervous he wees himself.

It's been a while since we've had an episode of the incontinence that once blighted our lives. But what if it comes back, right now? His change of food put a stop to it, but you can never be certain, especially as he often forgets he needs to go for a wee when he's stressed.

I have been asked a question. I didn't quite catch it, nor who asked it. I glance up to find everyone in the room smiling at me expectantly, awaiting a response. I make a guess at what was asked, assuming it was about Kevin. I'm relieved to find my response is not only appropriate, but also elicits some kind of delight.

The mother, wearing a smart dress that wouldn't look out of place on Princess Michael of Kent, seems stressed. She strikes me as rather brittle, while the father, who sports comfortable slacks and a country shirt, comes across as a mite pompous. I need to tread carefully.

The father takes only non-alcoholic beer. I join him, partly to endear myself, partly so I remain sharp and don't fall into the trap of making stupid comments to cover up my discomfort and desire to run away. Not for the first time, I am extremely grateful Kevin is with me and I can stroke his soft, if slightly dusty, fur. He allows me, if only for a fleeting moment, to slip into our shared world.

He adjusts the position of his head beneath my hand and swallows. I smile. My partner is telling a story about me. I am happy not to speak, and merely nod my head in agreement, adding colour to her story with a knowing look here or there. I am not sure I would have chosen to tell this particular tale. It makes me seem as if I am led around by Kevin like a hapless servant. I see us more as equals who support each other on our journey through life, but who am I to quibble? At least the parents find the story charming. The mother laughs and smiles at me, while the father suggests I shouldn't be dragged around by the nose, although he admits to being the same with his beloved sheepdog.

Ah, the sheepdog. I had, in the airless tension of the room, briefly forgotten about this furry complication to our visit. I fantasise about making my excuses to give Kevin a quick constitutional walk in the extremely well-kept garden, then slipping out the back gate and heading to the pub down the road. Kevin is in his element in a public house. He revels in the noise and the smells, the affability of the drinkers, the indulgences of the bar staff, and his tail-wagging happiness is infectious. I also have the impression he appreciates the constantly renewing clientele and the reinvention that it brings. Mind you, in a quiet bar he will happily curl up on my lap while I sip at a pint or two and watch the world go by in contented simplicity.

But I cannot slip away, and the stilted conversations

of the first encounter between a newly acquired boyfriend and her parents cannot distract me from an impending sense of doom. It is certain, unavoidable, that Kevin will be introduced to their, I am sure, extremely nice family dog. I have to accept that people, no matter how rational they seem in normal life, will always be adamant that Kevin—so small, so beautiful, so beatific and innocent in his charming expressions—could clearly never hurt a fly, let alone their beloved pet. This is despite not knowing Kevin from Adam, or rather from Adam's dog, if he had one.

I try to insist that their lovely, innocent and somewhat elderly sheepdog should be left in peace on the cool tiles, rather than exposed to this angel-turned-devil as soon as another dog appears. But my protestations fall on deaf ears. So I sit, awaiting the inevitable, sipping on my alcohol-free beer. I smile, I nod, I occasionally laugh on cue. There is a grand piano nearby. I would love someone, anyone, to go over and play it, just to bring some variety to the occasion and distract me from my thoughts.

Kevin's body is still pressed against my thigh. He is getting hot, almost uncomfortably so in the close environment of the Best Room. He licks his lips from time to time. I can feel his Adam's apple rising up and down on my leg every time he swallows. I wonder, not for the first time, if it can be at all comfortable for him to press his throat against me like that. I ask myself yet again why he endures it and doesn't simply adjust the position of his head, even slightly.

Maybe he doesn't want to lose contact with me. Maybe he needs the reassurance.

He certainly reassures me. Except that now, he is shaking. Does he need a wee? Has the dog of the house awoken from his slumber in a far part of the ancient rambling building? Can Kevin hear the soft pat of his feet or the slight creak of a floorboard? What horrors will he unleash when the sheepdog arrives? What grand social faux pas will he commit that I shall have to explain away, potentially for years to come? Will he bite their adored pet? If he does, surely it won't be enough to draw blood? Will he go into crazed barking mode and become so inconsolable and out of control I have to take him out of the room?

That has happened before, many times. In those moments, he can end up yelping and practically screaming, thrashing around in my arms like a fish hauled onto the deck of a boat. He has scratched me until he has drawn blood, even bitten me as he writhes in desperation to get at the object of his crazed hatred. Usually, in the midst of his madness, I catch someone's eye and they look at us with a mixture of stifled humour and bewildered incomprehension. Later, when things have calmed down and Kevin is restored to his normal angelic self, witnesses to his breakdown often drop hints he might benefit from some training. They look incredulous when I happily inform them he has already had plenty of it. While he is now much better than before (cue more incredulous looks and eyebrows pushed up even further), the general conclusion is some dogs have a problem with their own kind and there is not much that can be done about it. It's hardly satisfactory as an explanation, and I feel like a fool saying it, but there is little else I can offer.

— Shall we bring the two boys together, then?

I am jolted out of my reverie. I want to say: — No, of course not. Are you mad?

But I remember where I am and why I am there. So I say nothing. Then I tell myself the same lie I have told myself 100 times before.

Maybe he'll be fine this time.

— It's about time they met, adds the father. — If

they're going to be friends. I can't wait to see how they get on.

Friends? Friends?

I stare at him. He *is* mad.

The father pulls himself out of his pristine chair, upholstered in the same flowery pattern as the sofa, and ambles over to the door with a happy grin on his face. I tense up, mentally preparing myself to expect anything. The daughter, my partner, should know better than to allow this meeting to take place. But she smiles at me as if it is all the most natural thing in the world. I try to smile back, knowing the mother is watching me intently.

Everything feels forced. I can sense Kevin is stressed, potentially thanks to me. We both wait in anticipation. I feel as if the world is about to cave in. The heat rises in my body. The father places his hand on the latch. Kevin sniffs the air vigorously, bouncing his nose up and down with each intake of breath. With a click, the latch is lifted a centimetre. The sheepdog, slow and benign, pushes the door open with his head and ambles into the room, mirroring the gait of his master. Kevin's air-sniffing becomes frantic and his whole body is shaking with the effort.

Once the sheepdog is within six feet, Kevin growls, quietly but determinedly. I can feel the vibrations from his chest all the way up my arm. The sheepdog freezes, looks at me nervously, then stares at the father of the house as if looking for some guidance. Kevin growls again, this time slightly louder.

Without waiting for instruction, the sheepdog sidesteps and sits down behind a plant pot on the coffee table, ensuring it is between him and the angry house invader. It looks as if he is trying to hide himself from Kevin, although we all, including Kevin, can see him quite clearly. The sheepdog tilts his head and glances at me from around the pot. He seems almost proud of himself and his ingenuity.

We all laugh. The ice is finally broken. Kevin puts his head back on my lap and licks his lips, apparently satisfied that no further action is required.

CHAPTER 2

Many years before, when Kevin was much younger, I didn't realise his hatred of dogs was so intractable. When I first met him, he had endured a violent upbringing that he shared with other dogs. As well as being abused and neglected, he constantly had to battle for food and attention. I assumed—everyone assumed—that once he accepted that life was now okay and he could relax, his attitude towards other dogs would soften.

He did calm down, of course; otherwise, he would have been nigh-on impossible to live with. But, the initial euphoria he experienced when he began his new life wore off very quickly. He fell into what anyone would immediately recognise as a deep and lasting period of anxiety and depression that took him around two years to get over. Then, seemingly overnight, he became less frantic and stressed. His mood and spirit improved and he evolved into a bright, optimistic and cheeky young dog. By and large, he stayed that way.

The first time I thought I would test him in a meaningful way with other dogs was around one and a half years after his mental recovery. I knew he was still difficult. That had been made painfully clear by a few stressful and frankly dangerous encounters, when he attacked other canines without warning. But I thought I had seen a softening in his attitude, a mellowing of his nature, that made me wonder if he would be able to not only tolerate, but even have relationships with other dogs.

I am not talking about living with another dog, of course—that would be going too far, and I wouldn't want that for me, let alone for him. I would like him to have the odd friend or two we could see in the park, whether they be human, canine or ideally both. In reality, I simply wanted not to have to be on high alert anytime we found ourselves unexpectedly in the presence of another dog.

On many, many occasions, people suggested he might feel better around other dachshunds, as opposed to other breeds of dog. After all, dachshunds not only look like him, but also have the same kind of personality; one known to be unlike that of other canines. I didn't find that particularly convincing as an argument. However, due to a fear I might be wrong, and so end up inadvertently depriving Kevin of the chance to connect with other animals, and partly because I got fed up with being pestered about it, I relented.

ONE DAY, with much reservation, I decide to test their theory. I had, after much procrastinating, found a particularly active group of dachshund owners and enthusiasts in London that puts together meets and events in local parks. I hesitate over taking the plunge as the people who frequent dachshund meet-ups tend to favour the contraction 'doxie', making the dogs sound more like a disease than a rather charming breed of canine. And they dress their charges up in 'funny' costumes. Definitely not my cup of tea.

My notion of dog owning is simple: the dog lives with you; you feed and water them; you take them for walks and look after their wellbeing; and you build a companionable relationship. I see Kevin as an adult animal who deserves respect and the opportunity to express his own identify, and not to have one imposed upon him. Although it clearly isn't as straightforward as that: our relationship is so much closer and more complex than I could have expected, to the extent that it is almost impossible to tell where he ends and I begin.

For his part, Kevin just wants to get on with his life. This primarily consists of eating, sleeping, playing, long walks, scavenging for scraps on the street (if he can get away with it), chasing squirrels and cats, arguing with other dogs, curling up on the sofa (ideally pressed into someone's warm body), or wrapping himself up so tight in his blanket that any kind of movement is nigh-on impossible. Anything else is at best a distraction, at worst an outrageous imposition that elicits long and loud complaints.

He happily wears a coat or jumper, if the weather requires it. But I have always taken pleasure from his lack of tolerance of any kind of decoration, especially if it bobs about or gets in his way. He nevertheless has a full wardrobe of clothes given to us by well-meaning and doting individuals, including hats and all sorts of accessories he never wears.

I got my first taste of the other side of dachshund ownership on a visit to the international dog show Crufts, at the Birmingham NEC. I was surrounded by people who seemed to believe cute breeds should be dressed up like a cross between a young child and a doll. I saw more pink ballet outfits and deerstalkers on that crazy, fantastical day than in my entire life, either before or since. And it made me wonder for a moment whether my idea of what constitutes a dog–human relationship might be the one wide of the mark.

From the galleries of previous meet-ups, it is clear where the London dachshund group leans, with slightly blurry photos showing canines running around in an assortment of outfits. So it is with a degree of trepidation that Kevin and I walk across Regent's Park in London on a fine Saturday afternoon to join them. On the way, I remind myself repeatedly that the adventure is not for me but for him.

The group is initially hard to find in the vast expanse of grass and trees. I wander around a little aimlessly until I spot, or rather, hear them on the other side of a row of Saturday football pitches. That oh-so characteristic barking, mixed with the occasional panicked yelp that could only come from a dachshund, makes me realise we are not far away. Kevin's ears prick up immediately.

As we get closer, he starts darting ahead of me and straining on his lead. He is clearly agitated, increasingly so as we approach. I can now see there must be around 30 or 40 dachshunds of all shapes and sizes. Kevin is not yet barking, or making any noise other than the scrabbling of his paws on the ground, but it dawns on me that coming here might have been a huge mistake. His agitation is now reaching fever pitch. He glances at me, darts over to sniff my feet, then rushes back to the end of his lead and scrabbles once more. I wonder about picking him up and carrying him.

When we arrive, we see the dachshunds are, for the most part, dressed up, as hot dogs, bumble bees, Sherlock Holmeses, unicorns, cowboys, princesses and even a Superman. I think I spot a Spiderman too, although I fear I am becoming delirious. They are rushing about and creating havoc in the way only dachshunds can. Instinctively, I pick Kevin up. I glance about and read on a sign that the group is in the middle of a costume competition. After that, there will be dachshund races and other entertainments until late afternoon.

There goes my dream of a picnic in the park with a nice glass of something, surrounded by like-minded individuals.

I hang back and hold Kevin quite tightly in my arms in case he tries to jump to the ground. He is silent, but shivering; a sure sign of stress. I remember someone suggesting to me some of his overreactions might be caused by me holding him. The theory is that his vantage point of safety gives him a surfeit of confidence and fuels his maddened aggression. What they didn't know is that every time I have left him on the floor in these kinds of situations he has ended up biting a dog quite hard on some soft and delicate part of their anatomy, with all the imaginable consequences.

I squeeze him a little tighter as the costumed canines run about our feet and Kevin sniffs the air like a deranged vacuum. A woman with dark curly hair and a friendly face, dressed in comfy jeans and a striped top in the style of Blur's Graham Coxon, sees us and gives us a big, beaming smile. She then looks shyly to the ground before ambling over to meet us. I am hoping this will go well. She seems nice and disarming. As she approaches, she looks me in the eyes.

— Hello. You must be new here. Welcome to…

But before she can finish her sentence, Kevin looks down to find a stray dachshund in a bee costume by my feet. He instantaneously bursts into a screaming, yelping cacophony of barking, then tries to leap right out of my arms. I manage to catch him before he hits the ground. I attempt to calm him down, but he is already gone. There is no getting through to him. I simply have to take him away from the situation.

I smile apologetically at my nearly but not quite new friend, who had leapt back in surprise at this canine explosion, and turn on my heel. We are halfway back across the park towards the Tube station before he finally stops barking. Then he sighs deeply and looks up at me, with wide, innocent eyes, as if nothing has happened. I kiss him on the head like a child, stroke him, then put him down. He potters around on the grass and wags his tail happily.

Then we go back home, not for the first time with a little sadness in my heart.

CHAPTER 3

It is a beautiful Sunday morning in early spring, cold but bright. I am guiding Kevin, the meat-seeking missile, along the streets of Shoreditch, London. I feel a little ragged around the edges after a night out that saw me finally get home about two in the morning.

After the intensity of the party and the roar of the London streets, it was lovely to creep up the stairs in the quiet of the small hours, the only sound the click-clack of Kevin's claws on the wooden floor in the flat. Before I reached the door, I could hear the snort-pause-snort of his nose just the other side. I opened the door a fraction and he was straight into the gap, sniffing at my feet with outstretched nose, the rest of him still in the inside, his tail wagging so hard his rump swayed back and forth and his back paws slid on the parquet. He didn't look up at me, but sniffed at my shoes with deep intensity.

— Do you want to come out for a quick wee? I asked quietly, so as not to wake the neighbours.

He stepped back and looked up at me wide-eyed, his mouth half open, then bounced up and down on his front paws like a miniature horse.

— You'll have to let me in so I can get your lead.

I pushed open the door and stepped into the apartment. Bouncing all the while, he backed out of the way. I hadn't left the lead by the door and had to step over him to get it. He clearly thought I had already forgotten about going out, as he put his head over my foot with every step in an attempt to stop me going any further.

— It's okay, I just need to get the lead; we're still going out.

He stepped back and stood stock still. Holding his head up high and his body as tense as he could, he fixed me with an outraged eye and growled at me.

— I said it's okay. I'm just getting the lead. See, I said, holding it up and stepping towards him.

When he saw what I was doing, he melted in submission and slid awkwardly to the floor. He lay on his side, legs up and paws folded, licking his lips.

— It doesn't help me when you do that, I said, struggling to get him into his harness.

Once he was clipped in and his lead was attached, he flipped himself onto his feet in a single fluid motion and dashed for the door. However, he waited on the threshold until I was nearly next to him, to check I was really coming, before clattering his way down the stairs.

Outside, the cold air gave him pause. He looked at me with appealing eyes before running back to the door of our building.

— No way, you have to have a wee.

He stared at me a little defiantly and dug in his heels as I walked down the road.

— Come on, the quicker you have a wee, the quicker you can go back to your bed.

I pulled at his lead and he resisted, then instantly changed his mind. He sprang forward and ran all the way to the end of his lead, pinging off it and scattering himself across the pavement. He caught himself, then walked on, snaking around every bollard and lamppost, clearly looking for the most suitable spot to relieve himself.

Eventually, he settled on a place that seemed to me like any other, but evidently had the 'right' characteristics. He weed against it, all the while staring up at me and catching my eye, presumably to ensure I took note of what he was doing. I looked away. Once he had finished, he stood stock still, his leg still cocked, staring at me with his big, dark eyes.

— It's okay, we can go home now.

I'd barely finished the sentence before Kevin shot off back towards our building. He didn't ping off the end of the lead this time, but he stretched and strained at it with all his might and scrabbled with his paws, desperate to get back home as quickly as possible. He bounded up the stairs when I took off his lead and harness. I barely had enough time to close the door to the flat before he was already in bed, flipping his blanket over himself in a slightly frantic manner.

After a couple of tries, he got a little over enthusiastic and threw the entire blanket onto the floor. He stood up in his ring-shaped bed and stared at me.

— What?

I knew exactly what he wanted, but I love these exchanges. Kevin stared at the blanket, then back up at my eyes, then back down at the blanket.

— What do you want me to do?

He stared down at the blanket, then back up at me again. When he saw I was not moving, he lifted his head a little higher and opened his mouth, glaring at me with wild, threatening eyes.

— What? What do you want? I don't understand.

He glanced at the blanket, licked his lips, danced on his paws, then stared at me again, even more wild-eyed than before.

— What?

He barked quietly and bowed his head, all the while licking his lips. He repeated his little dance and glanced at the blanket.

— Okay, okay. I understand. I'm only playing with you.

I walked over and picked up the blanket. As I did so, Kevin wagged his tail and dipped his head. I lifted the blanket up like a sheet. He folded his legs and lay down on his side, curling himself up against the ring of the bed. I draped the blanket over him, leaving just his eyes and snout uncovered.

— Is that okay?

He stared up at me and licked his lips in a gentle, satisfied manner, before tucking his nose under the edge of the blanket and closing his eyes.

CHAPTER 4

~~~

Today, Kevin is much keener to go outside. The late winter sun reflects off his dark, shiny fur in iridescent colours. He delights at being out in the world. He still snakes around every bollard, but I get the impression he is doing it more by habit than anything else.

It is a fairly cold day, and windy at that, despite the brilliant sunshine, so I have dressed Kevin in his best red tartan coat. He looks faintly ridiculous as he skips along the street, his coat flapping from side to side. But there is no getting away from it: Kevin is extremely sensitive to the cold.

Maybe it is being so close to the ground, the large areas of sparsely haired flank open to the wind, his short sleek fur, or a combination of all three, but if he doesn't wear a coat in wintery conditions, he is soon shivering, unhappy, and demanding to be carried—not to where we are going, but home. At least dressed in this way, he is protected against the worst of the elements and we can have a walk we both enjoy. Plus he gets even more appreciative responses than normal, with people stopping to tell us he is simply adorable.

On this cold morning, the streets are mostly empty,

so he is left alone and concentrates instead on scavenging to his, if not my, heart's content. We make our way through the backstreets of Shoreditch, encountering the relics of a Saturday night out in the party capital of London. Among the smashed bottles, discarded cans and cigarette butts are potential treats for a scavenging expert who likes to leave no scene unexplored in the hunt for easy snacks.

I fret over whether he will be cut by the broken glass or twisted metal, especially if I pull him away from a bone or dropped morsel, so I try as much as possible to steer him away from likely hotspots before we reach them.

We meander our way to Hoxton Street, avoiding the worst of the bins and the dropped takeaway boxes.

A smashed window in an abandoned shop stares at the blank grey face of a low-rise block on the other side of the road. A hard-faced man with a Staffordshire bull terrier rounds a corner. Memories of Kevin being attacked burst into my mind. Thankfully, the man and his dog are on the other side of the road and Kevin is distracted, or wary, enough not to draw attention to himself.

As we reach Shoreditch Library, I ask myself what it would be like to grow up here, so close to central London. A few weeks earlier, a young woman was shot by accident as she picked up a takeaway order from the fried chicken takeaway on the next corner. She was only 16 years of age. A gang member opened fire on the takeaway with a submachine gun as they cycled by. He was also only 16. After he killed her, he simply cycled away.

I am not afraid to walk the streets of Shoreditch, even in the small hours of the morning, but I shudder at the thought of a young life being cut down so needlessly. It gives me pause. The attack was meant to be a reprisal after another gang member was beaten up by rivals, but that did not result in death so casually when I was living my teen years in the relative calm of Leicester. No amount of attitude or confident swagger will save your life if you are gunned down by mistake.

CHAPTER 5

For some reason, I am taken back to my adolescence. I was pushing 16, soon to be a black belt in karate and, due to some encounter long passed into school mythology, had a reputation of being relatively tough. For up-and-coming lads who fancied themselves as hard men of the future, people like me were easy targets for flashing a bit of muscle and grit. I was also a target because I was a painfully shy and reticent youngster, despite being able to handle myself physically with men twice my age. Any social encounter left me recoiling in fear.

One young man in particular decided he would show off by intimidating me, or whatever it was he was trying to achieve. He was one or two years below me, but was already tall and muscular in a way that suggested he spent an awful lot of time doing weights in the gym. Presumably knowing I was proficient in karate, he never took the risk of challenging me out in the open. In the confines of a crowded school corridor, however, he would try to shake me out of my daydreaming reverie by pushing and threatening me. I wasn't scared in the slightest, but I was nervous he would try something dangerous when I didn't have the freedom of movement to defend myself. Someone told me he carried a knife, although I wasn't sure they were being serious. I knew how to disarm someone, but not in a corridor full of schoolchildren.

I lived in daily anticipation of some form of escalation until, one day, he disappeared. He was simply no longer at school, and causal enquiries to friends or teachers yielded nothing. Then, someone told me my tormentor had killed a child while out joyriding. I understood that he and some friends were racing around the country roads near Leicester and hit a car head-on, killing the child in the passenger seat instantly, if not the mother too. He was convicted and sent to a juvenile prison.

I have to confess that teenage me was relieved he was no longer a threat, but I was shocked at that being the reason he disappeared so abruptly. A friend said at the time that something like that was always going to happen to him, but I didn't see it that way. If only he could have been steered towards a better life before he took one, especially that of a child.

BETWEEN SIXTH FORM college and university, I did not spend my gap year hiking in India or finding myself in Nepal while volunteering for a charity, much as I would have liked to if had I known that option was available. Instead, I worked to earn enough money to pay at least some of my way during my studies.

I landed a job as a clerical assistant in Leicester University Hospital, where I became aware, for the first time, of the depth of my naïvety. Being around grown-ups—actual proper working adults, with complex lives and responsibilities—woke me up to how much my friends and I were living in a childish bubble. We were completely unprepared for the outside world. In reality, we didn't even realise there *was* an outside world, apart from on television or in magazines.

It was a humbling experience. Treated as, and expected to act like, an adult, I worked hard and learned fast. The thing I took on board the quickest was how to be discreet, especially when running a general surgery and gastrointestinal outpatient clinic. Every Tuesday afternoon, people with all sorts of physical problems and ongoing complications turned up to my desk, handed over their appointment card and, rightly, expected to be treated with dignity and respect, no matter what I knew about them.

It came fairly naturally to me due to the respect my parents had demanded at home. But some well-placed words by a nurse as I began my first clinic behind the front desk drove home to me the importance of privacy, and of understanding. People came to the clinic in a fragile state, I was told. They often expected to receive bad news, or had to take onboard complicated and worrying information that would dictate the next few months, if not years, of their lives. I needed always to bear that in mind.

I had been working there for a few months when I asked one of the nurses what a special note on a case file meant. So that none of the patients sitting in the waiting room would hear, she whispered that it signified we were to expect a prisoner, escorted by guards. As soon they arrived, their notes were to be put to the top of the pile so they could spend as little time as possible in the clinic and get straight back to jail.

I didn't recognise the prisoner's name, or at least it was generic enough for me not to think anything of its familiarity. At some point, one of the department's appointment cards was dropped on the ledge in front of my eyes by the hand of a person in uniform. I looked up to see a downcast young man in the drab standard-issue outfit of a prisoner. He was chained at his hands and feet, and handcuffed to a guard on either side. It was the first time I had seen anything like that in real life and it was surprising enough, but then I examined the face of the young man whose name I hadn't recognised.

It was a face that hadn't changed one bit and yet was utterly transformed. This haunted, angular, distant young man was thinner than I remembered. He was no longer the bright, angry flame I had known before. Gone was the hard stare, the determined look, the challenge in his gait, the tough muscular body. Now he was a hollowed-out shell, a diffident, withdrawn young man whose instinct was to shy away from all contact and keep his head down. It seemed almost incongruous that he should be chained to two burly prison guards, when he seemed incapable of doing anything, let alone escaping them.

Only a few short years had passed; he would have been around 17 years of age. There remained some vestiges of the first flush of youth. In all other respects, he was completely different. But there was no getting away from it: he was my former school tormenter.

I duly put his notes to the top of the pile and watched him out of the corner of my eye, trying to understand. Who was he now? What had changed him so completely? Was it simply the fact of being in jail, or was there more to it than that? He was clearly injured enough he had to come for regular visits to a general surgery outpatient clinic. What had befallen him? I was naturally tempted to look in his notes to see what was wrong, but I resisted.

I was surprised I didn't feel some childish sense of victory over him. Instead, I pitied him. I wished things had turned out differently. If he had taken another path, perhaps he could have channelled his energy and aggression into something better than killing a child on a joyride. I was sure that, underneath it all, this young man, chained to two prison guards while he waited to see the doctor, was not fundamentally a bad person, or at least could be a much better one given the right circumstances.

I knew a lot of men at the karate club for whom life would have been much, much worse if someone hadn't introduced them to the demands and discipline of martial arts. I was violent in my early years at school, I suppose through a sense of frustration at trying, but failing, to find my place in the world. But I attended village schools at the time, where no one was lost to the system and everything got back to your parents in the end. Later, Karate smoothed off all those rough edges and set me on the path to becoming a measured adult.

Soon enough, my former fellow pupil was called in. I watched him shuffle, head still bowed, across the waiting room to the sound of his clanking chains. Then I was required to deal with something urgent. A while later, I wondered when he would return to the waiting room, and my desk. I was told he had already left, whisked away through a side door by his guards.

CHAPTER 6

KEVIN AND I TURN AT THE FRIED CHICKEN TAKEAWAY AND head towards Shoreditch High Street. I am still troubled by the young victim of the shooting a few weeks ago and the memories of that fateful day at the outpatient clinic, so I concentrate on Kevin darting about like a giant thunder fly. He is seeking and searching, although more relaxed now we have left the 1,001 temptations of Hoxton.

He is lost in his own world and clearly content, but I cannot stop myself reflecting on how events can affect the rest of our lives, like ripples through time. Kevin has suffered greatly from those who, for some reason, hate and misunderstand him. Leaving aside the causal violence and abuse from his previous owners, he has experienced numerous out-the-blue attacks by dogs that didn't see him as anything other than something to chase and destroy. And when we lived on London's Caledonian Road, he was regularly taunted and shouted at by unthinking drunks and teenagers.

I empathise.

A few years after I moved from university to the capital, I was still trying to find my place, as much within myself as in the outside world. There were things I wanted to be, facets of myself I wanted to project. I wanted to explore different ways of being, and hang out with different crowds. But I had been mocked and rejected every time I tried anything new in my youth. It held me back, even though I was now living in the land of endless possibility that is London, and knew no one from my past life.

I never went to the bars and clubs where I knew I could explore who I wanted to be. I never dared to meet the people who would help me wear the clothes, walk the walk, live the way I so desired, and make them my own. I was so afraid that I didn't even dare let myself start thinking about doing those things and going to those places. So much so I wasn't sure exactly what I yearned for, or who I wanted to be.

But it could have turned out so differently. When I was at university in the 1990s, a love of fine clothes was part of the territory. Many people dressed up for formal dinners in fancy frocks and black tie, topped off with a formal gown and a big smile. Day to day, it was hardly uncommon for a young student to wear a jacket and tie, or fine vintage clothes. It was the time of Hugh Laurie and Stephen Fry's *Jeeves and Wooster* TV series, with its fabulous tailoring, and the smart Cambridge footlights set had become ubiquitous on television and in the cinema. Many of us at the university at the time aped them and felt a certain responsibility to live up to their example. I revelled in all of that and lived it as well as I could on my limited means and equally limited imagination.

Down in London, however, things were different. The capital had not yet been transformed into a gilded playground for the rich and suspect. When I arrived, there were still IRA bombings, and Kings Cross was

MORE LIFE AS A DOG

better known for prostitutes and the ready availability of hard drugs than for trains. The air hung with danger. I loved that heady mix, however, and the rich kaleidoscope of possibilities it afforded, even though I typically viewed most of it from afar like a wallflower at a party: fascinated, intoxicated by what they see, but unable to join in.

But I did retain from university a love of dressing up like a relic of a bygone era, in smart trousers and shirt, topped off with a waistcoat and maybe a tie, all from vintage shops in Covent Garden. For a long time, I would put on my fancy get-up on a Saturday morning after a week of bland conformity in an office. Then I would drag Kevin around all the shops with me, him patiently watching the world go by my feet. Although he occasionally got extremely bored and would scrabble to get back to the cut and thrust of the busy London streets. I always knew that was my cue to put whatever I was contemplating back on the racks. I was clearly, in Kevin's opinion, spending too much time browsing and not enough time doing.

ONE FINE SATURDAY, I strode down the ramp, as it existed then, that led directly from York Way to platform 1 of Kings Cross station. This is impossible now ticket barriers have been introduced and all the rough edges of the station have been polished away. Kevin was trotting happily along beside me, head up high, quickly down to the ground, then back up again. The floor was too dirty and any detritus there too old to be of any great interest to a young dachshund, so he relished instead the morning walk and the freshness of the day.

I was dressed in a white shirt and narrow tie, pale

blue waistcoat in rust-brown pinstripe, dark trousers and shoes. I was not wearing anything controversial or, indeed, 'out there'; I was simply smart in a dandified way. And I was happy, enjoying the sunshine on a nice spring day and the freedom of the weekend.

Waiting by platform 1 was a train destined for Newcastle. A group of lads, dressed in denim or sportswear, or both, were heading towards me as they searched for their carriage. They were initially talking amongst themselves, but fell silent as, one by one, they noticed me. As our paths crossed, the lad in front, who had a hard stare and blond hair clipped down to his skull, twisted his mouth in disgust.

— You fooking poof, he spat at me. — Fooking poof, he shouted at the top of his voice.

The others joined in, shouting insults at me as they passed. Inside, I was shaking. There must have been at least six of them, and they were all tall, tough lads. It had been a good while since I had done karate regularly. Despite being in decent shape, I wouldn't have been a match for them if they had gone for me all at once. But I held my head high and walked on, neither acknowledging them nor returning their stares or comments, and certainly not running.

Once I had got over the shock and the adrenaline had died down, I was sad. All I was doing was walking through Kings Cross station in normal clothes, albeit not the kinds of clothes they chose to wear. What would they have done if I had dressed and acted in the way I wanted to inside? Would they have left it at hurling insults and foaming with barely contained aggression? More importantly, why did they act in that way? It would be tempting to say they were afraid of fine things and those who aspired to them, and wanted to hide their fear with bluster and violence. But another perhaps less reassuring notion might be that I, as a human being, displayed a kind of fear and vulnerability that both appeals and appals.

Still shaking inside, I glanced down at Kevin. He seemed perturbed, perhaps due to the noise the men made, but maybe also because of the reminder it might have given him of his past woes. Maybe this hatred he and I appear able to engender, puzzling though it is, is part of what binds us together. Perhaps it helps create a trust between us: I understand him and what he goes through. I also know how to protect him, and make him feel better in a way I'd desire if I was in his place.

But does this shared understanding also hold him back in some way? Does seeing my past experiences and fears mirrored in what he goes through mean I don't encourage him to be more adventurous, to be more out in the world and take on challenges?

Of course, when he is chased down by a much bigger dog that clearly does not see any kinship in Kevin, it is a different matter. When he was grabbed on the head by the jaws of a Staffordshire bull terrier in the middle of the street, I had to intervene. Otherwise, he would have been severely injured, or even died.

But when he is panicking and aggressive with a dog of his own size, could he overcome his feelings if I stepped back and let nature run its course? Surely a situation like that cannot go on forever? He must eventually calm down, even if just because he would tire and run out of steam. After all, he lived with other dogs in his youth, and one hears countless stories of dogs becoming used to cats and developing a tolerance towards, if not an actual relationship, with them.

But arriving at that point would require the other dog in the equation to be patient and not rise to provocation, even in extreme circumstances. Do such canines exist? I have not had too much difficulty in coming across people who think their dog is like that, but it is much rarer to find one be so benign when they are put to the test. And what if Kevin tries to fatally wound the other dog? He seems to have no limits once the red mist descends.

CHAPTER 7

I AM REFLECTING ON ALL OF THIS AS WE REACH Columbia Road Flower Market. We stop a few hundred yards away, regarding the mass of trees, bushes, plants and, above all, flowers before us. Vans line the narrow entrance to the market proper, their doors flung open, revealing plants of all kinds arranged like soldiers waiting to pile out and join battle. Cars are parked in all manner of ways and all manner of places. And people, lots of people, fill up every space on the street and crowd around the local pub, that serves both as a last-chance saloon before entering the fray and a point of refuge for those returning from the battle.

At this hour, the flower market is in full swing. Actually, it has been since four in the morning. In reality, we are late, even though it is only just past nine. Not too late, however, for the East Asian tourists taking pictures, nor for the casual Londoners who fancy some flowers for the week and a nice Sunday experience, the category into which Kevin and I fall.

It has always puzzled me that the organisers choose to host the two lines of flower stalls on the narrowest part of Columbia Road. It is flanked by late Georgian terraced houses on one side and a school and a pub on the other, before petering off into east London street life. The houses are no longer for living in, but rather shops or cafés. The former are stuffed full of art, trinkets, leather goods, furniture, antiques, cards, stationery and so much more, while the latter offer a tempting selection of bagels, prawns and calamari in little pots, sandwiches, cakes and, of course, fancy tea and coffee.

All of this means the area is packed to the gunwales, as they say. The stalls themselves heave with blooms and plants of every kind, and many others you've probably neither heard of nor seen before. The stallholders offer their wares in thick East End and Estuary accents at the tops of their voices, and the heady aromatic mix of clashing bouquets and greenery wafts like a heavy Victorian perfume. It adds up to a combined assault on the senses that sweeps you along in its wake, transporting you to another time. The crush of people milling back and forth searching for bargains and inspiration in equal measure ensures that, when the attendance is at its greatest, it is impossible to walk comfortably by oneself, let alone with a child or dog. Yet I have, rather foolishly, brought Kevin with me.

But I love the place. I would also love a cup of calamari rings and Thai jelly, along with a double espresso, to start my day. My canine companion also adores shellfish, indeed all the riches of the deep. This could present its own problems if and when I buy some. He also loves sniffing flowers. He often runs up to beds in parks and plants his nose fully in between the petals, breathing in deeply. He never bites them, or at least not now he is grown up. He just appreciates them before running off, although it can be hard to convince a keen gardener that a quick sniff is all he wants with their beloved florals.

Weighing all this up, I contemplate the crowd, hesitating over whether to go in. Kevin looks up at me in expectation, then over at the market, then back up at me. His tail is wagging.

I know full well I will have to carry Kevin. With him in his tartan coat and me in my thick winter jacket, both seeming appropriate when we left, I am sure to get hot. It takes some time to organise Kevin and his flapping coat so we are both comfortable and I can move properly.

But he doesn't want to wait for me to finish. He tries to scrabble up my leg, causing his coat repeatedly to get in the way. He glares at me impatiently as I arrange and rearrange him with increasing frustration. He tries to settle down into my arms, but cannot get comfortable. He stands up with his front paws on my hands and his back legs pushing into the crease of my elbow, then tries again. All his struggling, and my fighting with his stupid coat, has made me hot and bothered. A bead of sweat rolls down my spine, and my hair, tucked under my thick flat cap, is damp. I take off the hat, but stuffing it into my jacket when I am already carrying a full-grown and nearly full-size dachshund is not so easy.

By this time, we have entered the heaving, noisy throng of the market. I accidentally elbow a much smaller man in the back of the head as I try to put my cap away. His instantaneous anger turns to purring delight, however, when he sees the black pools of Kevin's huge eyes staring placidly back at him.

— I'm sorry, I mutter.

The man beams at me before turning back to negotiate with a stall holder over some rather beautiful begonias.

I am still arranging myself when Kevin licks my nose. I recoil and trip over the edge of a flower stall, falling through the open door of a shop and nearly landing flat on my face. The quiet of the calm interior is shattered by my boots slapping on the wooden floorboards. Several people eyeing up handmade jewellery and expensive greetings cards stare at me as if I were talking loudly in a library. I spend a quiet moment regretting my over-ambition in coming here with him on a sunny day, even if it is a rather wintery one, then pull Kevin and myself out of the shop. The bead of sweat running down my spine is now a stream. I am at my least urbane and sophisticated.

We work our way back through the crowd. I try to relax and not let the situation get to me, especially as the heat of carrying Kevin on my arm in the mass of people adds to my sense of claustrophobia. My canine companion, on the other hand, is happily taking in all around him, serenely catching the aromas, floral or otherwise, that waft up to his gently bobbing head.

We pass a shop selling maps painted on to metal sheets. For the umpteenth time, I think I should stop and buy one. I then look down at serene, happy Kevin and change my mind.

How would I get the thing home?

There is the jeweller's I keep meaning to go into to buy someone a birthday present, but again we walk by. I contemplate heading down the charming side street by the Royal Oak pub, but I study the potential pathways through the crowd to get there and decide against it.

I pause and see out of the corner of my eye Kevin's bobbing head swing gently to the left. He is following a smell as it snakes through the air beside his nose. Still tracking it, he drops his head down and carefully lays his chin on the shoulder of a woman standing by a flower stall. She pulls away from him in surprise, but bursts out laughing when she sees who, or rather what, has made such an intrusion into her personal space.

Unusually, she doesn't turn around to look at me, but talks to Kevin directly, smiling at him and asking him if he likes the flowers. I smile too, happy to watch the interaction between them, then turn away and carry Kevin further down the street.

We reach the calamari and prawn vendor, and my hunger and hangover instantly go into overdrive. This is neither shop nor café, but rather the front window of a terraced house, through which snacks are sold in polystyrene cups. More is prepared on tables just behind, in what must once have been the living room. Kevin licks his lips repeatedly as we wait our turn. Together we gaze at the rows of containers filled to the brim with delicately battered *fruit de mer*.

I am too distracted by hunger to take proper notice of what Kevin is doing. I assume he isn't that bothered by food as he ate heartily at breakfast. I adjust his position as we reach the front of the queue so I can pay and pick up my order with one hand and hold him away from me on my other forearm. I opt for both prawns and calamari. This means juggling two polystyrene cups, but I think ahead enough to squeeze a little lemon on both before attempting to pick them up.

The server is amused by Kevin and we have some back-and-forth about him. The light jolliness of the moment, despite my sweating and the growing tiredness in my arm, makes me happy I brought him with me. I could have taken him back home after our morning constitutional walk. But I always have a strong sense of guilt when I have been out the evening before, especially when I have also worked long hours all week. So I try to make sure we go out at least three times a day, and that one of those walks is substantial.

The smiles and jollity don't last long, however. Not for me at least. We shuffle down to the edge of the counter with my two polystyrene cups of deliciousness, held by two fingers of my one free hand. On my other arm, Kevin is struggling to reach one of those plump, fresh prawns, so tantalisingly close to his snout.

I always forget how long he can make himself, especially when he elongates his neck and pushes against the inside of my elbow with his back paws. With all this stretching and straining, the muscles in my left arm are now fiery hot. Yet we are only at the midpoint of the market, with no chance of me putting him down without either retracing our steps all the way to the start or pushing through the crowd to the other end. There are simply too many people around for him not to get stuck under everyone's feet and start panicking in the enclosed space of all those legs.

So, I have no choice. I have to carry him and the two polystyrene cups, while preventing him sticking his nose in one or both. I straighten my back and stretch out my chest so I can push Kevin as far to my left as possible. I stack the two cups, then delicately pick them up with a precise finger arrangement that leaves no room for error. We push into the crowd with my two arms as far apart as I can manage. But Kevin has now wrapped himself around my torso and stretched out his neck. His nose twitches up and down furiously, his eyes bulge as he strains every sinew to get close enough to snatch a morsel of joy.

Of course we bump into people in this ridiculous arrangement and I curse myself under my breath. My hope of not sweating profusely has gone out of the window and my only goal is to make it from the crowd without dropping Kevin, the cups or both. I bang my head on an immaculately aged doorframe and a prawn drops out of one of the cups. Kevin lunges after it as it falls past his face. He nearly takes me and the cups with him before I can straighten myself and stop him plunging head first to the floor.

— Can you just stop it, I hiss tersely.

A woman turns around and scowls at me. Her perfect red lipstick breaks into a broad smile as she takes in the scene. She laughs.

— You've got yourself into a right pickle there.

I smile back, trying to look relaxed, despite the sweat on my brow and the rivulets running down my back. I lift the cups up to her height in a bid to get my coat to sit properly on my arm. Kevin wraps himself around my neck, getting ever closer to the food. The woman laughs again and I try to look amused. I have given up on controlling the situation and try to pretend this is normal. Kevin's fur is hot against my throat, however, and a sense of soft strangulation only increases the tension in me.

— C'mon, stop it, I say.

I see him, in extreme close-up, give me a crazed glare out of the corner of my eye. His breath is rasping. I wonder how much longer I can hold him. Mercifully, we reach the end of the crowd. The commotion we are causing has caught people's attention and a path is cleared for us to get out of the mêlée.

We break out into the open in a stumbling mess. I drop Kevin to the floor as gently as I can, grateful to see him land evenly on all four paws and bounce lightly on his pads. I do not fare so well, however. I trip over something unseen. As I do, half of the contents of the polystyrene cups spring out and land on the floor. Ready as ever, Kevin leaps into action and scoffs down his prawn and calamari booty with an indecent enthusiasm, leaving me to shout resentfully.

— Oi!

But it's too late. There's nothing to do but stare ruefully at the half-empty cups.

CHAPTER 8

I SHUFFLE ALONG A LITTLE DISCONSOLATELY AFTER OUR accident with the seafood. I didn't want to eat that many prawns and calamari, but that's not the point. Kevin looks up at the cups feverishly, then at me with pleading eyes to make sure I am noticing his stares. He tries to trip me up by placing his head over my foot and biting my shoelaces as I walk, in a vain attempt to convince me to give him at least one more morsel of calamari.

In reality, he shouldn't have eaten even one. Calamari and prawns are bad for his stomach. But there is nothing I can do about that now. I don't even want to go back through the flower market and see what is on offer, or along the side of the pub to look at the fancy furniture and antique shops. There are nice food stalls down there, where I could have bought lunch and a drink, but none of it appeals anymore.

I am not annoyed at Kevin. He is only following his rather cheeky instincts. I am not even that frustrated with myself, but rather feel stupid at having created a situation where things would evidently go wrong. I was not optimistic in buying the calamari and prawns, but foolhardy. I know how he is, and that he has to be carried in a crowd. I do allow, however, that I had forgotten just how packed the flower market is at that time of the morning.

I trudge on, lost in self-criticism, munching occasionally on a cold prawn or ring of calamari, trying to ignore the desperate, pleading creature huffing and puffing by my feet. A creature who, once again, will not let me wallow in self-pity, but drags me back to the present. I try to suppress a smile, but can't. I stop and turn to him. He looks up, swallows nervously and sits down. He glances from the polystyrene cups to me and back again.

— Will you stop begging, just for one minute?

He stares hard at the remaining cold seafood, then back at me.

— You weren't supposed to have any in the first place.

He stops glancing at the polystyrene cups and fixes his stare on me. He shivers slightly.

— They make you sick. You're probably going to have diarrhoea today after scoffing down all that. I'm not going to make it worse by giving you some more.

— Excuse me.

Unbeknownst to me, a man in a smart hat, with a rather cold and resolute expression on his face, is right behind us and wants to get past. I realise my 'conversation' with Kevin may seem a little odd. I watch the man stride down the road with a degree of embarrassment. In the meantime, Kevin has taken matters into his own hands and is getting himself ready for another leap at the polystyrene cups.

— Oh, no you don't, I say, lifting them out of the way. — There, I add, polishing off the last pieces and throwing the cups into a nearby bin. — Now it's over. They're all gone and we can forget all about them.

Kevin stares at the bin disconsolately, snorts, then,

after a brief pause, carries on walking. He has his head down and is slightly ahead of me. I was enjoying our little interaction. I hadn't wanted it to stop so abruptly. But what did I expect? I am the one who threw away the cups.

We continue along Hackney Road. I wonder what to do now. I had envisaged walking the long way back home via the main road but I am not sure I want to go back yet. We could head for Victoria Park, although it is quite a way off. I look up at the sky. Not a cloud in sight. I smile at Kevin, then take off my jacket. I also take off his coat, causing much tail wagging and licking of lips, and throw them both over my arm.

— Let's enjoy the sunshine and go for a walk, eh? No plan, no direction.

Kevin trots on ahead, then skips on three legs—a sure sign of joyfulness. Just as we pass Hackney City Farm, my phone buzzes. It's a text from friends who live further up towards Dalston. Would I like to join them in Haggerston Park in half an hour for a picnic and a drink? Meet us at the Whiston Road entrance, they add.

That is the nicer end of Haggerston Park, with a colonnade that recalls a mythical long-lost stately home, and rather attractive flower beds. I check the time, although I am not sure what difference it would make; we have just established we have no plans for the day. So, I text back to say we'd be delighted. I'm happy to see these friends. Kevin is particularly keen on them. The only question is what to do for half an hour, as we are only five minutes from the rendezvous point.

After some cajoling, I persuade Kevin to retrace our steps and head back down Hackney Road to buy food suitable for a picnic, and some hopefully cold beers. The nearest shop is Turkish, so has a selection of delicious-looking meze. Even better, the owner doesn't mind me taking Kevin in with me. I raid the fridge for beer, pick out the freshest of that morning's Turkish bread and a few dishes. All the while, Kevin stands as close to the door as possible, ready to shoot out. It is as if he cannot bear to be further inside the shop. He pulls hard on the lead while I am trying to pay.

— Can you just relax? We'll be out in a minute.

He stares up at me with an offended expression. Once back outside, he clatters along, ready for anything, scavenging for scraps, launching himself from one side of the pavement to the other. I have no idea what he thinks he is doing, or where he thinks he is going, but he is clearly very excited. I wonder if he smelled some dropped food by the side of the shop as we entered. The further we get down the road, the more he relaxes his pace and walks, rather than runs.

We get to the park a little early, so I perch myself on a wall by the entrance on Whiston Road. Now extremely calm, Kevin sits next to me like a statue. I stuff our coats into the cheap blue carrier bag with the food and beers. I look around, first for my friends, then at anyone who passes by. Kevin, on the other hand, stares single mindedly at the traffic on the main road at the end of the street. I watch him from time to time, wondering what he is thinking about. He occasionally looks up and catches my eye, before going back to regarding the traffic.

I love these quiet, convivial moments, watching the world go by and sharing the anticipation of what's to come. It is so rare we do nothing together during the daytime. We are always busy or on our way somewhere, or at least I am. I end up dragging him along in my wake. We hardly ever get time for just the two of us.

Kevin is sitting in front of me, at the end of his lead. He turns and catches my eye again, then pulls himself up onto his feet. He trots over to me and sits back down on his haunches, leaning his rump against my feet and his body against my legs. I reach down and fiddle with his ear. I rub the tuft of fur at the back of his head, under the ridge were it meets his neck. He licks his lips happily. I forget all about the sweaty frustration of our morning, the dropped seafood and the impending diarrhoea that will inevitably strike once the prawns and calamari have made their way through his delicate system.

Now, here, on a side street in Hackney, it is just him and me, whiling away the time as the cars pass by at the end of the road and the kids run and scream in the park. There is a gentle breeze in the shade of the plane trees and for now at least, all is calm. It is in these perfect moments that I sense the invisible thread strung between Kevin and me. It seems as if it has always been there, binding us irrevocably together long before we even knew each other. Times like these pull on the thread, drawing us ever-closer, collapsing the space between us down to nothing. I think about picking him up and giving him a hug, but I don't want to break the spell.

Our friends appear at the end of the road. Recognising them instantly, Kevin springs to his feet and runs forward. The moment is gone.

CHAPTER 9

Kevin gallops to the end of his lead. He ricochets and spins around like a top even before I get the chance to stand up.

My friends call excitedly to him and he bounces up and down on his front paws like a little horse. They love Kevin as much as if he was their own and have looked after him once or twice when I've had to go away. The male, Andy, often rolls around on the floor with him, and has declared on numerous occasions that Kevin is the coolest dog in the world, especially when he puts on his aloof, disinterested airs. The female, Isobel, is a naturally loving and warm person who makes everyone feel at ease, helped by her wonderfully happy smile and big, endearing eyes that captivate with the merest glance.

Isobel has a feature that Kevin loves particularly. It makes him go straight over to her whenever he sees her sit down and beg to be picked up. If she relents, depending on the company, he clambers up her until he is able to lean on what may be described as her ample bosom, then hooks a paw into her cleavage. He looks so satisfied and happy, he reminds me of a child seeking the warmth and heartbeat of their mother.

I should underline that he doesn't do this with anyone else at all, or even try to. The first time he did it with Isobel, she was a little shocked and unsure how to react. What did it say about her, she wondered. Should she be offended, or amused? The faintly Benny Hill aspect to the whole thing didn't help. Now she is more used to it, especially as he is clearly so happy when he settles into her décolletage; so much so, he often gets his way if she is wearing a low-cut top.

Today, Isobel wears a buttoned-up blouse and jacket, and we are in a public situation. Kevin will be disappointed but there will be plenty of other things to distract him. Now I think about it, they both look rather dressed up and in good spirits.

— Are you off anywhere nice later?

— Well, she says, and laughs guiltily. — We said meet us in the park for a picnic.

I glance down at my blue plastic carrier bag, bulging with snacks, beers and our two jackets. I wonder if I've inadvertently made a mistake.

— But we didn't say the picnic is for someone's birthday.

— Oh, I say, somewhat crestfallen.— Will they mind if I come along too? Is it anyone I know?

I now deeply regret not dressing properly and simply stepping out in whatever clothes lay closest to me in the rush to take Kevin for a walk. I contemplate leaving our friends and going home.

— No, says Isobel. — He's a friend of mine, but you've never met him. Actually, we won't know anyone apart from him.

I must look sceptical, as she quickly adds: — We don't really have to get involved. I can just say hello and happy birthday, and then we can have our own picnic. To one side.

— Oh, okay then. Well, if he doesn't mind, that sounds good to me.

— Stop it!

I look down to find Andy crouching and Kevin with his front paws on one of his knees. He is sticking his long pink tongue deep into Andy's ear with an enthusiasm that borders on the obscene.

— Stop it, Andy cries out again in mock horror.

— You don't have to let him do that, I say.

I wonder if I should pull Kevin away from him.

— I know, he says, looking up and smiling. — But it's his way of saying hello. And I haven't cleaned my ears this week. They need a good rummage.

— Ugh, Isobel says, staring at me wide-eyed and with not-at-all mock horror. — Disgusting.

I screw up my face. I pull Kevin away and he looks disappointedly up at me.

CHAPTER 10

I AM DEEPLY UNCONVINCED BY ISOBEL'S BELIEF THAT everything will work out fine. How can we have a separate but vaguely connected picnic next to that of the birthday boy? It's as close to crashing a party as it gets without actually doing so. I don't imagine the person in question would be so unsophisticated as to say anything other than it's fine, so he doesn't come across as a spoiled child, but I don't imagine he will be too thrilled.

Kevin, of course, has no such reservations. The realisation that a picnic is taking place in our direction of travel is enough for him. Picnics equal delicious food, all neatly presented on the ground. He hurls himself towards this one at full tilt. He doubtless believes that, if he can get into open space sufficiently ahead of me, he can grab something and scoff it down before I can stop him.

I, on the other hand, am both wise to his stratagems and wary of getting us off to a bad start, especially in view of our questionable status at the picnic. I lock his lead as quickly as I can and hold him steady where he is. Feet splayed, he huffs and puffs at me over his shoulder, glaring with obvious frustration and barely concealed anger. He scrabbles impotently at the grass, then turns back to me, still angry. I sigh back at him and shrug my shoulders.

— Wow, he's on form today, Isobel says.

— He can smell a mini sausage roll a mile off, I say, tugging again at the lead like a deep sea fisherman trying to land a catch. — And I'm in no mood to have him ruin a birthday picnic before we've even had a chance to crash it.

The closer we get, the more I can see that these are not one's average picnickers. This is the trendy East End crowd, wearing arty clothes in an array of colours and textures. Gingham abounds, both in the picnic cloths and the dresses. The talk is slow and deliberate, as if every word is being weighed for its import and impact before being issued out into the world.

The emotions may be muted, but the colours and extravagance of the cookery are not. This is high-level picnicking. I note that no one has done anything so crass as to bring packets of hummus and stuffed vine leaves in a plastic carrier bag from the local Turkish corner shop.

Afternoons, mornings and even entire days have been spent in making cakes, sweet and savoury dips, and salads. I even spot homemade vol-au-vents, all presented in self-consciously retro and fancy Tupperware. Not a thing out of place, not a single pre-made product. I assume all this effort comes with the expectation of a weighty pause for appreciation from onlookers at presentation, to be followed by appropriately effusive compliments and questions on the recipe and the origin of the ingredients.

In contrast, I look like a stray from the wrong side of the tracks among this crowd. But at least my friends are well-dressed, even if they, wisely, didn't bring anything to eat. I take Kevin to one side and we sit while my friends make their greetings. Cringing over my inadequacy and lack of preparation, I wish I was neater and tidier, cleaner, more interesting and more original. I also wish I was poised and sorted enough to be able to muster up half the fancy titbits the real guests seem to have thrown together with the simplest of ease. My bulging blue plastic carrier bag screams of last-minute low-rent purchases. I hide it as well as I can behind my leg, and look at no one.

Kevin, on the other hand, does not care for any such anguished torments. He is happy and delighted that there are new, potentially weak and manipulable, people to beg from. And if that doesn't work, all that food, so lovingly prepared and presented, is surely within reach of his searching, seeking, questing snout.

In my shame, I fancy for a second that Kevin will, like a scene from a 1970s sitcom, slip his lead and head straight into the middle of the picnic, destroying and scoffing everything, causing mayhem and ruining the self-conscious gentility of the occasion. But my rational mind eventually gets the better of me and I settle down. I nevertheless pull Kevin closer so he will sit comfortably by my side.

I surreptitiously take a can of beer out of my bag and open it. The pfffft of the ring pull causes Kevin to flick back his closest ear, but he does not break his stare at the main group of people for even a second. Presumably he is intently weighing and reweighing up his odds. After a sip or two of lukewarm beer, I notice everyone else is drinking wine from nice plastic glasses. Wine that is kept chilled in travel ice bags. These people are the same age as me, I determine. How is it that they are so much more sophisticated and poised than I am?

When I was at university, one person in particular sticks in my mind as being both of those things. A person who, as predicted at the time, went on to have a stellar academic career in the arts. I was a craven, bewildered working-class boy; she was the very epitome of everything I could never be. I saw her, in some ways, as one might regard the emergence of fireflies just after sunset: a thing of beauty one could admire only from afar.

But that was then. I was an ungainly student, as were almost all of my peers. That there might have been one or two among us who seemed to have descended straight from heaven was acceptable. But now? How could I, in my thirties, still be so disorganised, so un-together, so immature that I haven't started living a fulfilled and conscious life?

CHAPTER 11

I watch my friends chat to various people and sample the delicious-looking titbits, happy to sit alone drinking beer. I am hungry, but I dare not embarrass myself anymore by taking out my second-rate morsels.

After a while, a tall and striking woman in a vintage psychedelic-print dress comes over and introduces herself. We chat a little. I am awkward and uncomfortable. She notices and finds that awkward in turn, but we stiltedly try to have a conversation, for my part so as not to make a mockery of her kind efforts to be welcoming.

I am uncomfortable not only because I feel out of place and desperately uncool in my standard clothes, with my standard shop-bought snacks and, above all, my standard personality, but also because I've spotted a cockapoo on the other side of the main body of the picnic. I wouldn't mind so much, but Kevin has spotted it too. I can feel him quivering as he sniffs the air frantically, interspersing his efforts with the odd snort, like an old judge scoffing at a ridiculous intervention in his court.

My interlocutor senses that my agitation and distractedness are linked to Kevin. She asks about him and

I explain a little about his antipathy towards other dogs. Bit by bit, as we explore the topic further, I express my concern that I have validated and exacerbated his difficulties with canines due to my reticence to expose him to further risk of injury, or to cause insult to animals and/or their owners. She sees the dilemma, especially as I explain that Kevin is often the aggressor, jumping in before the other dog has a chance to do anything. She suggests a controlled environment might be the best way to at least see whether his issues are ingrained or simply learned. I have no sooner concurred with her pleasingly scientific approach than she suggests that right here, right now—in short, this very picnic—might be such an environment.

With a sense of panic and a strong wish I had kept my big mouth shut, I demur. I am not comfortable even being at the picnic, let alone with crossing one of the red lines in Kevin's relationship with the outside world. But she reassures me cockapoos are the ideal dog for such an experiment, due to their naturally placid nature. She is so reasonable, so calm, so sure, so logical. I dare not disagree, for fear of sounding over protective and mistrustful.

— What can go wrong? she asks.

I can think of 1,000 things that have already gone very wrong very many times over the years I have known Kevin, but I merely smile ironically and raise my eyebrows, more to register my doubt with myself than to contradict her.

— They'll both be on a lead, she says. — They'll both be held. There'll be nothing they can do to each other.

I must still look doubtful, as she adds: — You might be surprised at Kevin, and at yourself.

I resist the temptation to say: — And so might you.

But I don't want to prejudice the situation any more than I am already with my cynical attitude and obviously tight body language. I am also trying not to introduce any conscious or unconscious bias and so influence Kevin's behaviour. After all, I know full well that if I hold him fearfully, he will be more stressed and anxious, and more likely to act badly, than if I hold him calmly.

So I deliberately loosen my grip and talk to him in a laidback, light-hearted tone. The woman then gets up, straightens her short dress and heads over to the owners of the cockapoo. She crouches down next to them and speaks in a whisper.

For the first time in a while, Kevin takes his eyes off the other dog and looks up at me. He licks his lips. His eyes look a little apologetic. This, I tell myself, is a good sign. I smile and ask him if he is okay. He wags his tail happily, glances away to the other side of the park, then stares at me with an adorable expression. There is the possibility he is, with his looks and demeanour, trying to tell me he does not want to meet the cockapoo and would rather leave. I choose to believe, however, that maybe this time, finally, he will have a positive interaction with another dog. And wouldn't that be an enormous relief?

I fantasise that this could be the start of a whole new life for us both. I imagine him making friends with this dog, then them becoming regular walk partners, and after that Kevin learning to appreciate other dogs and befriending them too. Maybe, if it all goes well, we could end up in a situation where he can accept the society of dogs without a second thought. Maybe, just maybe, we could go back to the Dachshund Day and, if not put him in a stupid costume, at least let him enjoy being in the company of his fellows. I think back to the friendly lady with the happy smile and the Graham Coxon-style outfit. I smile warmly down at Kevin and he wags his tail again.

I look up. The woman in the psychedelic dress is pointing at me. The couple and their cockapoo strain their necks to look at us. I smile and give a small wave. The couple smile back in a knowing and understanding way that reminds me of the parents of a perfectly behaved child looking pityingly at those of one who have just done something regrettable and symptomatic of a wider failure in their education.

I am embarrassed and feel faintly patronised, so I look down at Kevin and talk to him. He has a put-upon expression on his face that he wears when he seems to know that something of significance is about to happen, but he has no idea what. Anticipation is what that is and, well, I feel that too. I purposefully decide to reject all preconceptions and simply let happen whatever unfolds over the next few minutes.

Then I recall that I did not come to this picnic on my own. I glance around to locate my friends. They are nowhere to be seen, at least from my spot in the grass. I have a brief flash of panic. Perhaps I am looking for them to offer some sort of reassurance or validation, or simply to support me in the potentially stressful moment to come. Maybe they have been watching us and have decided to scarper before the inevitable ignominies begin.

The psychedelic woman stands up and pulls her dress down. For a fleeting moment, I wonder if she regrets having worn that specific outfit to a picnic. When she's walking along a street, I am sure it looks fabulous and feels fabulous to wear. Sitting in a chair, she must look great in it. But the inelegances of navigating a sit-down picnic in the grass are not its forté. Nor that of her solid, chunky heels.

Did she also feel out of place and awkward when she arrived? Is that why she chose to come over to me? Did she want to speak to a kindred spirit?

Perhaps. On the other hand, she is evidently extremely comfortable in her skin and with her choices in life. Maybe she detected my obvious sense of inadequacy and merely felt sorry for me. After all, she is very empathetic.

Maybe she simply wanted to make me feel better.

All such thoughts are banished from my mind as I see she has taken the lead of the cockapoo and is bringing him over to me. It is too late to back out now. I try not to brace myself for the worst and instead attempt to void my mind.

I also reassure Kevin, who has noticed the dog is heading towards him. My canine companion has resumed his intense sniffing and snorting, and his bouncing head causes waves down my thigh, into which he is now vigorously pressing the full length of his body.

The other dog is nearly with us, and my heart is in my mouth. But the psychedelic woman makes it all seem so very natural. She doesn't introduce the dogs to one another or make a fuss. She simply sits down, rather awkwardly in her chunky heels and short dress, invites the cockapoo to sit next to her and engages me in conversation about presumably the first thing that pops into her head.

She impresses me with her forethought and poise. I follow her lead, talking brightly and happily and letting the conversation flow this way and that in a chatty manner that I hope is infectious. I glance down at Kevin from time to time, while maintaining the run of the conversation. He sniffs the air, but there has been no great change in his demeanour. He does not seem more stressed than before, beyond a slight increase in the frequency of his sniffing. After a few moments, he tucks his nose into the space between his body and my thigh—a sure sign he is relaxed enough to consider going to sleep.

I raise my eyebrows and look down at Kevin out of the corner of my eye in a theatrical manner so our psychedelic tamer of wild beasts will notice. She smiles and nods in satisfaction, before returning to our conversation. The cockapoo does, as advertised, seem very relaxed and unbothered by the small canine curled up by my side. He also settles and lies down next to his adopted friend.

After a while, we permit ourselves to talk about the situation. I express amazement at what has occurred.

— Maybe it's just a question of the right circumstances, the psychedelic woman offers. — And you feeling at ease and ready to give him your lead in accepting other dogs.

— Indeed.

— And perhaps it needs to be the right dog. I know cockapoos are particularly easy going. So maybe that helps.

It all gives me much food for thought. I recount the episode to Isobel and Andy when they turn up out of the blue and sit down next to us. Kevin looks up at their arrival, but soon re-inserts his nose into the space next to my thigh. I introduce her to them as my dog saviour. Together, we discuss mood, context, transmitting feelings, pheromones and the notion that humans are just as susceptible to projected emotions, atmosphere, and reactions as dogs, but we don't see it in the same way. We venture that it all gets a little lost in the context of language and visual cues.

I now feel relaxed and finally part of the picnic, no longer worrying about my awkwardness or whether Kevin will go crazy at any minute. I think he might even be asleep. He is certainly warm and soft under my hand.

For his part, the cockapoo looks around the park. He has his forepaws on the psychedelic woman's knee to get a better view. He looks for all the world like a furry statue at the gates of a large mansion; a lion, as drawn by children. He is no longer interested in Kevin in the slightest. It all feels like progress.

A man with a broad smile and happy face comes over to say hello.

— I've heard you brought a beautiful dachshund with you and he's going through some sort of therapy.

I laugh. — Yes.

Kevin wakes up at this and looks at the man, who gazes back happily.

— He certainly is lovely. What a charming face. It's hard to imagine he have an issue with other dogs.

— Yes, I know. When he's like this, he doesn't seem the type at all. Like butter wouldn't melt in his mouth. The problem is he was very maltreated when he was a puppy. And he lived with two other dogs at the time and they apparently did not get on one bit.

— Oh dear, the man says. He shows an exaggerated sad face to Kevin, reaches over and strokes his ears. — How did he get past all that to be so adorable now?

— Well, it was a lot of work, to be honest. He was depressed for a long time.

— Oh dear.

— He used to suffer a lot from anxiety, so my then-partner and I tried to give him a calm and loving environment.

— It must have worked, the man says, looking up and smiling.

It dawns on me, partly because Isobel is gesticulating wildly behind his back, that this man is the birthday boy, and is making the rounds of the guests.

— I'm sorry, but is it your birthday we're here to

celebrate? I came to see my friends and I'm something of a gate crasher.

The man smiles and nods.

— Happy birthday, I offer.

— Thank you. How long did it take your lovely friend here to get over his rotten past?

— Quite a bit of time, actually. Maybe two years for him to calm down fully, but it was worth the effort.

— I can see that, he says, gazing back down at Kevin.

— We did our best to help him have no reminders of the past.

— Oh, how?

— Obviously, he changed his home and location when he left with us, but we also made sure he had new toys, and a new lead and blanket, so he had nothing left from his previous life.

— That makes sense, the birthday boy says, stroking Kevin's ear again.

— And we changed his name.

— Oh yes? So he wasn't always called Kevin? The man looks up at me in surprise.

— No. He had another name. We didn't like it. And it didn't suit him at all, I say, pulling a face as if I have smelled something awful.

— Oh, right. What was his name?

— Jasper.

The man looks at me for a moment, then says quietly — My name is Jasper.

At that precise moment, Kevin notices the cockapoo again and starts barking maniacally.

PART II
ON THE ROAD AGAIN

CHAPTER 12

We had no choice, in the end: we had to leave London.

Kevin and I had been living very happily in a flat share in Greenwich, just behind Maze Hill station, but sadly, that arrangement came to a rather abrupt and unpleasant end. Prior to that, I had been travelling around Central Europe and the Balkans for a few months and, on my return, we'd needed somewhere to stay at short notice. But rental prices had risen so steeply in the capital during my absence that finding somewhere on our own, particularly in an area where we wanted actually to live, was out of the question. Furthermore, I was, following the 2008 financial crash, in a very precarious position. I couldn't be sure of when or indeed whether I would earn regularly, let alone have enough to pay for our lodgings.

So I scoured endless listings for flat shares in an ever-widening circle of central and then semi-suburban London, just to cater to our budget. When I factored in the need for the place to be dog-friendly, it reduced the possibilities down to only a handful of places within the whole of the M25.

I do understand that people's lifestyles in London

do not typically lend themselves to having a dog, but many landlords, and even freeholders, severely restrict pet ownership. They occasionally allow a cat, but rarely a dog. Many times I had to hide the fact I had a dog just to visit a property, let alone rent it out, and now was no different. I found myself with the shortest shortlist of potential places for us to rest our heads at very short notice.

The first and pretty much only place on the list that truly caught my eye did so simply because the occupants sounded interesting. However, they were hesitant about letting me even visit the flat when they heard I had a dog, only relenting when I explained Kevin is small and charming, does not need a huge amount of exercise, almost never barks and drops only the tiniest of hairs. In the end, they were swayed by him being a dachshund, an idea they found adorable.

A FEW DAYS LATER, we step off a train from London Bridge on a wet and wintry evening, in an area of the city neither of us knows at all. Due to the inclement weather, Kevin is dressed in a sensible coat. He excitedly skips along the back streets from the station, exploring every wet nook and cranny as he trots by, all the while making sure he avoids any large drops or puddles.

He tries to walk past the house when we arrive and it is only with much protest and reluctance I manage to drag him back to the gate. I am disappointed to find it is a basement flat. I assume it will be damp and dark. But of course Kevin doesn't care. Once I convince him to follow me, he bounds down the steps and wags his tail enthusiastically as he waits by the door, looking up at me every other second to check whether I will open it or ring the bell.

When he realises we will be waiting for someone to let us in, he goes to sit down. Then it occurs to him that will make his bum wet. He therefore reluctantly half-stands, and gives me a somewhat peeved stare. We don't have to wait long, however, as the door is soon pulled open by a very small and very smiley young man. He gives me a cheery welcome that becomes even bigger and cheerier when he sees Kevin eagerly wagging his tail.

— Well, hello. Aren't you gorgeous? he says, bending down towards Kevin. He then looks up at me, and adds: — And the dog's not bad too. Come in. You must be our potential flatmates.

We are ushered into a very cosy living room and offered a place at one end of the sofa. Our host takes the armchair and his current flatmate, a warm, open and equally small woman from Liverpool, sits at the other end of the sofa. She folds herself into a position that reminds me of an emerald brooch worn by my grandmother.

I carefully clean Kevin's paws and take off his coat before placing him on the sofa next to me. His is cold, so I hold both of his front paws in my hand. The three of us humans then embark on a long, rambling and extremely funny conversation that ends with a very clear indication that the room at the back, which I discover faces out into the garden and is neither dark nor damp, will be mine. My future flatmates warn me they will, of course, be seeing other people, but they frankly doubt any of them would have as charming and sweet a dog as Kevin.

— Looking forward to living with you, little Kevin, the young man calls after him as we leave. — And we might let you bring your owner.

. . .

WITH THAT, we embarked on a life together on the edge of Greenwich Park. I rediscovered a pleasure in living, brought about in part by the good fortune that Kevin and I could go for long, long walks in a beautiful place with endless horizons. This rekindled my love of parks and nature, and of a life I had not known for a long time. I began to crave the countryside of my youth and to question, for the first time in about 20 years, whether I needed or even wanted to live in London.

Our little oasis was wonderful, especially as we could play in the garden or, more commonly, walk just a few minutes to one of the most beautiful open spaces in any city in the world, let alone in London. Or we could wander along the Thames, either west towards the City or further east and back in time to the capital's industrial and maritime past.

Just after we moved in and before that renaissance fully took hold, I had sunk, post-Balkans trip, post-financial crash, to my lowest point since my divorce, or perhaps even since my mid-twenties, when suicidal thoughts had been a daily occurrence. Indeed, there were times early on in that flat share in Greenwich Park when I wondered whether I could, or even wanted to, carry on living. But little-by-little, I saw another path, especially when Kevin, one fateful morning, placed his head in my hand and gently led me outside and into the sunshine. It was also then that I began to appreciate I was living with two people whom I liked very much, and who liked me in return.

Yet life is made up of a series of interconnected yet inherently unstable equations. The female member of our happy little household found love, so she moved out to live with her girlfriend. That put my remaining flatmate into a bit of a tailspin, where he saw his life only in the starkest and most negative terms, and questioned what he was doing if he had no one to share it with.

When we asked the landlords to pay for essential repairs, they dug their heels in, saying we had necessitated the work because we didn't look after the flat properly. And that was when things came to a head. My erstwhile positive, funny and happy-go-lucky flatmate lost his temper in such a dramatic manner that, no matter how much placating I tried with the estate agents, the landlords terminated our contact and we were left with a month to find somewhere else and move out.

So, there we were, Kevin and I, homeless and facing a stark decision over our future. Either we attempted to find another flat share, which may be equally unstable and almost certainly less advantageous than the one just pulled out from under us, or we make the Big Leap and leave London for good.

In the end, it wasn't much of a decision. I had, deep down, wanted to move back to Stamford, in Lincolnshire, for a long time, even though I had only really thought about it seriously in the previous few months. I knew it would offer us both the life we wanted: lots of open spaces, lovely places to explore and an accepting attitude towards dogs. And so, a few weeks later, we found ourselves standing among dozens and dozens of cardboard boxes on a bright sunny morning in a new, lovely flat, all to ourselves and far from the Big Smoke. I saw the excited shine in Kevin's eyes as we together searched for his food, water bowl and packet of treats, and I knew we had made the right decision.

CHAPTER 13

Kevin already knows Stamford, so it doesn't take him long to get used to it and find his preferred walks. My favourite—and his too, judging by the way he skips along when he knows we are going there—is to do the circuit around Burghley Park. We always start at Bottle Lodges, then head up the path towards the park proper and the 16th century splendour of Burghley House. Before long, Kevin is driven slightly mad by the sheep and their droppings. The latter are, to him, edible titbits, and the idea of chasing something big and fluffy has an eternal appeal.

Today, once we brow the hill and drop into the lower park, the wind picks up. I adore how it lifts his ears and blows them out flat to the sides. With his determined, fixed expression and his fancy new brown sheepskin coat, he looks the very incarnation of a World War II flying ace, battling against the elements as he seeks out his enemy.

He catches my eye, then flattens himself even further into a sleek black arrow, trotting resolutely into the wind. The sun is shining brightly and the day, despite being early spring, feels warm and optimistic. The sheep are dotted about the park, milling here and there, grazing on the grass and the bottom branches of the trees until they are utterly flat.

As usual, there are other dogs out on this splendid morning, but they are far enough away to be no bother to Kevin. He even seems to have lost interest in trying to eat the sheep droppings now we are further into the park. He is content simply to do the rounds.

At the knot of trees where we could continue up the hill to the main part of Burghley Park or turn back towards home, I stop. I want to see where Kevin fancies going. Not noticing, he walks on, up towards the house, and soon hits the end of his lead. Leaning forward on the cord, he doesn't turn around but glares over his shoulder at me, wild-eyed and determined.

— Do you want to go this way? I ask, starting back towards home.

No response, other than to look ahead, up to the park proper, then back at me.

— Are you sure you don't want to go home and snuggle up in your bed?

I shouldn't really be discouraging him, but I am in two minds whether I want to continue. We have a lot to do today and I want to get on.

I move a fraction of an inch in his direction. He scrabbles to climb up the hill towards the main park, his claws scratching on the tarmac path. He pants with the exertion. I relent and follow him. At the main gate he waits patiently for me to open it, then launches himself forward at full pelt, as if to make as much progress as he can in case I change my mind. He needn't worry. I have resigned myself to a long walk.

We head straight on towards Burghley House, glimpses of which show through the avenue of still wintry ancient trees. Kevin is in his element now: the lord of the manor surveying his domains. Or maybe it's that he can smell the herd of deer in the field at the bottom of the park. Hundreds of them live on the estate, sometimes descending to the main park at dusk to take possession of the space they and their ancestors have enjoyed for centuries.

Kevin leads me on and on. It is clear by the time we reach the fork in the path that leads either up to the house or down to the bottom field, and therefore to the deer, he's had an ulterior motive all along.

— No way, we're not going down there.

He stops and stares at me over his shoulder, giving me a dirty look.

— Absolutely not. You only want to chase the deer, which you cannot do, and, in any case, the path is all wet and muddy. You'll get dirty and you'll hate that.

He looks down the path towards the bottom field, then back at me.

— No, it's either on towards the house or we go back home. We're not going that way. That's final.

Kevin doesn't budge, so I tug on his lead.

— Come on, time to go back home.

He leans away from me so I can't easily shift him. He stares at me with his head tilted back, giving me a manic look, as if he might bark at any second.

— We're not going down there. We haven't got time. Anyway, I told you, you'll get dirty.

Kevin pulls at the lead once more and digs his heels in, leaning even further away from me. My heart sinks as I realise we could be in for a very long haul. I have rarely met a person, let alone a dog, who can be as stubborn as Kevin once he sets his mind to it.

Then, without any warning, he stands up as if nothing has happened and happily trots past me to go back home. As I follow him, I am left wondering what on earth changed in his mind. Why did he give up?

The rest of the way back, he trots contentedly, just

in front of me, much more at ease now than he was on the way there. He even ignores the sheep and their droppings as we pass.

CHAPTER 14

BACK HOME, HE RUNS AROUND THE FLAT AT FULL TILT TO get himself warm: we were in the shade on the way back from Burghley House and the breeze was sharp and much colder than when we had left.

He bolts down the corridor and into the living room, then snatches at a toy in his basket. If he grabs one, he worries it in his mouth before throwing it across the room, but if he misses, he huffs in anger and pauses to stare at the toy in question. Either way, he then dashes back down the corridor to the kitchen, where I am getting our things ready for the day. As he reaches the kitchen, he slides to a halt with his front paws splayed, his mouth half open, his eyes wide, staring at me so I will notice him. As soon as I do, he locks eyes for a second, then gallops back down the corridor, snatches at a toy in the basket and repeats the cycle.

After a while, panting and sufficiently warmed, he ambles back to the kitchen and takes a long draught of water from his bowl. Then he trots off, licking the excess water from his lips, as if it's all entirely normal behaviour.

In the meantime, I have almost finished getting

everything together. I have a treat or two, Kevin's dinner for tonight, a water bottle, his breakfast for tomorrow morning (we may stay away overnight) and a huge carrot, in case he gets desperate. I also have a blanket, a warm coat, and a couple of his favourite toys.

Satisfied we are ready, I wander into the bedroom to find him. He is tucking himself into his bed for his afternoon nap.

— Hey, you can't go to sleep now.

Kevin stops and looks up at me, puzzled and a little put out.

— We're going out.

Rather than displaying his usual irrepressible enthusiasm and bounding over to me, he shows no change in expression and does not move an inch. Clearly the idea of going out again so soon does not appeal in the slightest.

— We're going to London, to see friends.

Kevin gives me a nonplussed look and resumes clambering into his bed. He starts to throw his blanket over himself so he can go to sleep under it.

— We're going in the car. You can sleep in there.

He stops for a moment, wags his tail a couple of times then continues putting himself to bed.

— Sadly, you don't have much choice, my lad. I have to take you with me. But you'll have a nice rest while I drive. And you like these friends a lot. They always fuss over you and hug you. Mind you, most people do that.

Kevin is now halfway under the blanket and trying to ignore me.

— Come on.

I lift him out of the bed and carry him, floppy in exaggerated resignation, back to the hall to put on his lead. He lies motionless on the floor while I get his lead together, expressing the most passive form of protest in his armoury.

I wonder why he is not more excited about going in the car with me, when he always used to love it and would leap up at the mere mention of the word. But then I remember on the last couple of occasions I had to brake very hard, not yet being used to the less decisive driving one finds in Stamford versus the punchy style in London. He ended up being flung off the seat and into the footwell.

Of course, I felt terrible at the time, but I assumed he was, ultimately, fine. After all, once he got over the shock, he simply gave me a dirty stare and resumed his place on the passenger seat, settling back down to doze. But I have to admit that, since then, he has taken to bracing himself when I slow down. It seems like a bad review of my driving technique, although I make sure I drive as smoothly as possible for him.

It is in these moments I feel most keenly my inability to explain to him what is happening and why he doesn't need to worry. It also occurs to me that I am perhaps over-confident in my driving abilities and he does indeed need to worry whether I will, without any warning, brake like a maniac.

I frown and stare at him. He is still lying motionless, like a put-out dog statue. But I can't leave him there. He has to come with me. So I delicately feed his harness over his inert, floppy body and clip the lead in. That usually has him accepting we are going out and jumping to his feet, if not with enthusiasm then at least with a best-foot-forward attitude. But he remains prostrate on the floor. He follows me with his eyes as I wander around the flat finishing getting everything ready. Still no sign of movement.

I finally announce we are ready to go and reach down for the lead. Kevin instantaneously flips himself onto his feet with an action that recalls a fish on the deck of a boat. He stands to attention, wagging his tail and staring at me fixedly.

— So, you do want to come?

He barks at me a couple of times, while still wagging his tail.

— Are you ready, then?

He wags his tail even harder, all the while locked onto my eyes with a fixed stare.

— Let's go, then.

I make for the door and he fusses around my feet, trying to grab my shoelaces. I presume he wants to be first to the door, although he may simply be trying to stop me walking to make it impossible to leave. When I open the front door, all doubt is banished when I see him hurls himself down the stairs with utter abandon, practically hanging himself on the lead when he gets to the end.

He rushes out the back door and into the yard behind the house, heading straight for the nearest tree for a wee. That's another thing I have noticed: Kevin has picked up that, now we live in Stamford, we drive more often and for longer than before, so he always makes sure to relieve himself before he gets into the car. If he doesn't realise what we are doing, I tell him to have a wee, something he can now do to order. I watch him and smile proudly to myself about his ability to learn new tricks, in spite of the well-known phrase. Then I wonder what it must be like to live inside his mind. I decide it must be a very busy and intense place.

Once he has finished, he heads straight for the driver's door of our racing green 1996 Vauxhall Astra, staring first at the lock, then back at me, then back at the lock, wagging his tail and pretending to paw at the door for me to open it. He never scratches the paintwork—I told him off for doing that several years ago and he's not done it again. Not even once.

MORE LIFE AS A DOG

I open the door and he leaps straight onto my seat. He then deliberately and carefully steps over the gear stick and handbrake before settling himself down in the passenger seat. He presses the curve of his back into the cushion and licks his lips. Then he folds his paws over the side of the seat next to the gear stick and places his chin on them.

I watch him for a moment, enjoying the little ceremony that he performs in the same way every time we take the car out. He stares up at me without moving his head from its resting place. He is so cute I want to give him a kiss on the top of his head.

— I wonder: do you want your blanket?

No reaction, other than a faint, almost imperceptible wag of his tail. Grabbing his purple cover from the bag I chucked on the back seat, I shake it out fully and throw it over him. He doesn't seem very pleased with what I have done. He gives me the impression he is merely tolerating the blanket's presence. After a pause while I get ready to set off, he picks and pulls at the blanket with his teeth, dragging it this way and that until he gets frustrated and throws it into the footwell.

— I guess that's a no, then.

I start the car and drive away.

CHAPTER 15

LIKE SO MANY DRIVERS WHO SEEM TO BELIEVE THEY ARE always in a hurry, I am in the habit of imagining I am in a race against another version of myself who set off from the same spot at the same time, and must beat him to our destination at all costs. Revelling in the made-up chase, I dice with the traffic and the speed limit, trying to get from A to B in the shortest time possible.

Today is no different. Once out of Stamford, I pick up speed, going faster and faster as we head to the A1. I barely slow down as we reach the entrance to the main road to London. I quickly glance in the mirror on the approach to the two busy lanes of traffic heading south, then perform a racing gear change as I switch lanes between a truck and a slow-moving car.

What on earth am I doing? Why am I in such a hurry? Am I afraid of being late? I shouldn't be as we are not expected at a particular time. But I seem to think I should be the first to arrive anywhere, like the child in class itching to put up their hand. But is it actually more serious than that? Am I reckless? Do I have a death wish?

It is a rather sad admission that my repeated toying

with suicide during my twenties left me with rather a jaundiced view of life and my participation in it. But my unease with existence goes back further than that: in my late teens, I nearly died.

IT HAPPENED at my first karate club. I was not yet a black belt, but close to it. Our sensei had asked me and another up-and-coming lad of similar size to demonstrate a technique to the rest of the class. We had never performed it before, but he said he would show us what to do. In seeing us learn the moves, the others would get the idea.

I think he chose us because we were more technically proficient than most. We weren't the strongest, nor the fastest, but we were clean in our movements and that often gave us an edge.

It turned out the technique was extremely difficult to grasp. It involved a complicated series of movements, the overarching idea and direction of which was not at all clear, at least not to us. I thought I was the only one having difficulties, but it turned out my co-demonstrator was equally lost. Our sensei tried every which way to explain what he wanted. Then we had another go.

But, with a slip and a twist, my fellow demonstrator kicked me in my middle with such sudden force it lifted me off the ground. I went into shock and dropped to the floor. I couldn't breathe. My body simply wouldn't respond. As the oxygen ran out, my chest became tighter. My heart rate slowed. Yet still I couldn't make myself breathe.

This must have occurred over just a few seconds, but I remember wondering, with a terrible fear, how I could force my lungs to work. Nothing came to mind.

The tightness increased, but I stopped panicking.

Somewhere, in the deep calm of me, I knew I would never breathe again. It would all be okay.

My heart raced, then slowed to a standstill.

I lay on the floor, an awkward mess of legs and arms, unable to move. I gazed at the white painted wall and the brown wooden plank at the edge of the dojo.

A tight band constricted my chest.

No more struggling now. Nothing more to worry about.

Everything faded to grey.

So this is how I go.

The thought moved slowly across my mind, then came to a standstill, like a train arriving at a station.

Then there was nothing. Just blankness, emptiness. It was as if I had been simply switched off and all the power had drained away.

I could see nothing, hear nothing, feel nothing.

No shining lights, no revelations, no life flashing before my eyes.

I was simply no longer there.

The End.

AND THEN, the world rushed back in. I was pulled upright and sweet, sweet air flooded my lungs. The room spun around me. My heart pounded in my chest with a terrible force. The sweat sprang from my skin. I breathed more deeply than I had ever done before.

A headache slammed into me. Too weak to stand, I collapsed again to the floor.

But I was alive. Back from the dead. Back from the void.

THAT MOMENT WAS something of a full stop for me. I realised, at 17 years of age, that I was mortal and capable of having everything taken away from me in an instant.

In a physical sense, I recovered from the event quickly, but I was left with the abiding belief that everything is meaningless when one is standing face-to-face with death. And death can come at any moment. How is it worth planning for the future, thinking of the consequences of anything at all, when you've looked into the abyss and you know there is nothing, absolutely nothing, there? There is not even blackness, just the absence of existence.

The End.

I have wondered many, many times if that is why I drive so carelessly, because I know it won't make any difference if I live or die. In some ways, I am already dead.

CHAPTER 16

Back on the A1, I slow myself down. I am not already dead. I have Kevin in the car. He is very much alive, and very much my responsibility. He does not deserve to go out in a blazing car crash. I tell myself over and over again: I will drive more carefully. I will chauffeur him to London like a VIP.

We head down the A14, then on the M11 towards Walthamstow. Except I am not the ideal chauffeur: the petrol warning light has just blinked on and the needle is into the red.

— Not to worry, this car can go on for miles, I say breezily to Kevin.

He was sleeping, but now he opens an eye to regard me, presumably to work out if I am saying anything of consequence. He closes it again.

I am confident. There must be a petrol station somewhere along the M11. After all, I don't recall a significant stretch of motorway anywhere in the UK that doesn't have some sort of services somewhere along its length. Or is it that I have spent so long living along the A1, dotted as it is with petrol stations, restaurants and stop-offs every few miles, that I have become complacent?

Then I see a sign that makes my stomach clench.
No Services on the M11.
Worse, the sign says the next services are several miles along the M25 in either direction. Even if we could make it to either of them, that would take us far, far out of our way.

I stare at the needle. We are deep into the red. I know that that is a little deceptive in this particular Vauxhall Astra and the last quarter is very long. Plus, I am pretty good at eking out petrol for many miles.

However, that last quarter may be long but it doesn't last forever. And there is a limit to how much one can conserve petrol while driving on the motorway. I nevertheless try my best, slowing down to just below the speed limit and ensuring the revs remain as low as possible.

But I know it won't be enough. We need to find a petrol station, and quickly. I look down periodically at Kevin. I am glad he seems oblivious to my tension, although he is usually the first to pick up on it.

We pass another sign. We still have a long way to go before we get to London. Even driving slowly, with the other cars and vans whizzing past and buffeting us in their wake, I am going to have to take drastic action.

I try to look through the hedges and trees lining the motorway as we pass to see what I can of the townscapes that lie beyond. I hope I can spot a petrol station close by, but each time I do, it's either too late to come off the motorway or I am far from an exit. I try not to panic, but it's not easy when I see the needle is closer to zero than I have ever seen it before.

CHAPTER 17

We pass Epping and Loughton. This is, more or less, London. Surely I can find a petrol station before we run out completely.

Just as the M11 sweeps into the North Circular via four lanes of endless, roaring traffic, the car goes light. I feel the engine stutter. Kevin sits up and stares at me, clearly worried. I have no time to calm him down. We are in the fourth of the four lanes. We need to get off the road as soon as possible. Fearfully flicking my eyes from the road to the rear view mirror and back again, I somehow, miraculously, manage to guide the car, like a glider coming in to land, from lane to lane, threading our way through gaps in the traffic as we go.

I head for a bank of grass right next to the entrance to an enormous roundabout. By the time I cross the final lane, the engine is completely dead and I am rolling on momentum. I can see in my mirrors four lanes of vans, taxis, cars, trucks and buses bearing down on me. I pray there is enough energy in our metal carcass to mount the grass and get off the road.

Kevin is standing on the seat and staring at me intently. He is clearly perturbed. He falls backwards as we strike the kerb, bounce over it, land on the grass and roll up the bank. Relief comes over me in waves, but my elation is cut short when I realise that only three wheels have made it off the road. I sit there, immobile, hoping and praying the car holds position and doesn't trundle back into the oncoming traffic.

After a minute that seems to last an hour, I decide we are relatively safe and allow myself to look around. I take in for the first time the enormous scale of the roundabout feeding lane after lane of vehicles into the gigantic, endless flow that is London traffic. It would be impressive, if I didn't have to get out of the car and do something about our perilous position.

— But what should I do? I ask Kevin.

Fortunately recovered from our crash landing, he is sitting on his haunches on the passenger seat. He glances from me to the traffic thundering past within inches of our window, then back again with a sort of nervous wonder in his eyes.

— I guess the first thing is to get the car off the road.

I reach for the door handle. Kevin panics.

— Don't worry, you don't have to come with me. At least not now, anyway.

I look over my shoulder at the relentless flow of traffic and resolve to get out as quickly as possible. A terrible roar fills the car as soon as I open the door a fraction. I hover for a second. But I have no choice, so I step quickly out, slam the door shut and slip around the back of the car.

I try to ignore the traffic thundering by and stare at the back wheels. We are so nearly on the bank. Just one wheel is hanging off into nothing. Bracing my shoulder against the back of the car, I glance up. Kevin stares at me nervously from the front seat. His desperate look strengthens my resolve. I try to heave the car onto the grass. But it's very heavy going. I have to lift the entire back end off the kerb and onto the grass and I am, frankly, struggling.

I look around and wonder if I can leave it like that, but it's clear we are far too close to the road. All it would take is a truck to be slightly off course and there would be a huge accident. Kevin and I would be goners, if not very badly injured.

I can't stop myself dwelling on the image of Kevin trapped in the car while a huge lorry ploughs into us. Shuddering right to my core, I determine to try again. I lean all my weight into the car, but I just can't get it high enough off the ground to push it all the way up onto the bank. I am about to give up when a car screeches to a halt right behind us and two big and clearly very tough lads jump out.

— You stuck, mate? one of them demands.

— Yes. Yes, I am. I ran out of petrol and couldn't make it all the way onto the grass. The car's too heavy for me to lift on my own.

— No worries, we'll give you a hand.

Without waiting for a reply, the two huge lads brace their shoulders against the car and the three of us push and push with all our might. After a moment of seemingly futile effort, the car suddenly pops up and onto the grass, rolling gently to safety. As it drifts away from us, I see Kevin's worried face appear between the headrests. He catches my eye and I wish I could give him a hug. Then I fearfully wonder if the car will continue all the way off the bank and into the road on the other side. But it soon glides to a halt in the long grass. I give him a big smile to reassure him.

I turn back to thank the two lads, but they are almost back in their car.

— Thank you so much.

— No worries, mate. Good luck.

— Oh, before you go... do you know if there's a petrol station nearby?

The slightly bigger one stops and stands up, one foot in the car and one on the grass.

— Yeah, it's just over there, he says, pointing across the eight lanes of traffic and the massive roundabout. — You'd have to cross this and the road on the other side. You can't see it, but it's there, behind the trees.

— Thank you.

Without any further delay, they slam their doors and reverse at full speed back into the traffic. They screech to a halt, then race off, joining the tea-time mass migration. I contemplate the empty space where their car had been, and their simple kindness in helping someone in need.

I peer nervously through the trees and wonder whether the bright yellow sign I can see peeping between the swaying branches is what I am looking for. I remember I need to check on Kevin. I go over to the car and stand by the passenger door. He has clearly been awaiting an update. He is standing tall on his front paws with a furrow on his brow. He stares at me intently through the glass.

— I've found a petrol station. Or at least, I know where one is.

I look over again towards the trees and wonder if it is really possible I can cross eight lanes of traffic on this side of the roundabout and another eight lanes on the other side to get there. Then come back again with a full can of highly flammable liquid. And what exactly will I do when I get to the petrol station? What if they don't have any jerry cans?

A little deflated, I look down again at Kevin through the window. He still looks nervous and disconcerted. Should I leave him here? Or should I try to cross 16 of the busiest lanes of traffic in Western Europe with a black and tan dachshund?

It seems a ridiculous idea, but then I think about leaving him in the car while I fetch the petrol. My mind immediately revisits the horror vision of a truck ploughing into the car with Kevin stuck inside, this time with me returning from the petrol station, full jerry can in hand, witnessing the accident from the other side of the roundabout.

I sigh at Kevin through the window. He licks his lips nervously and half wags his tail. I have no choice. I have to take him with me.

CHAPTER 18

Once Kevin is out of the car and safely clipped into his harness, I turn towards the road and the lanes of massed traffic roaring by. Understandably, he is reluctant to approach the edge. He stares up at me fearfully.

However, miraculously, the first four lanes are empty. Realising this won't last for long, I try to pull Kevin out onto the tarmac. He resists, hard, so I sweep him up into my arms and briskly walk across, reaching the central reservation just as the next onslaught of vehicles brows the hill and bears down on us.

I clamber over the dirty, dusty, rubbish-strewn barriers of the central reservation with Kevin still in my arms. I don't want him to injure himself on whatever may be hidden in the long, ragged grass, but the job of getting over to the other side is made that much more difficult by my having not picked him up cleanly when we started our eight-lane highway dash. His feet and legs tangle in my jacket and more than once, I nearly trip over and drop him.

Finally, we're on the other side of the central reservation. The four lanes entering the roundabout are also, just when we need them to be, mercifully free of cars. We scuttle across to what I discover as we get closer is a small path, partially hidden by the roadside barriers, next to an untidy and overgrown hedge. Why the path is there, and where it is supposed to lead in this dust-blasted roadscape, is a mystery. But I am grateful there is a space there wide enough for me to stand comfortably.

I am also able to put Kevin down on the path, but as soon as I do so, I see it is strewn with plastic waste and broken glass. I pray he is careful and put my trust in the soft and spongy pads on his paws. They seem to allow him, judging from many past experiences, to walk freely on all sorts of surfaces that would lacerate my much more vulnerable feet.

I remember a time, however, when he walked through broken glass and a shard got stuck in one of his paws. I didn't realise until I saw him limping and whining in pain, holding up his paw and looking at me with imploring eyes to do something. I had to lay him down on the pavement to take a proper look. It was only after I had, as delicately as I could, cleaned the blood from his paws that I could see the sliver of dark glass standing proud from the side of one of his pads. I took hold of it, causing him to whimper, and pulled at it with all my might, while trying to be as controlled as possible.

It pained my heart to see his thick, dark blood oozing over the rough black skin of his pads and trickling down into the golden brown tufts of fur in between. Kevin lay back, watching me and trying to relax, but he soon recovered himself once the shard was out. He licked at the blood, then at his wound, while I made sure the glass was out of harm's way and couldn't hurt another passing animal. After a minute or so, he was satisfied and flipped back onto his feet, and we resumed our walk.

CHAPTER 19

On the roundabout, we follow the narrow path around the outside. The cars whistle by just a few feet away. I doubt we will be so lucky in crossing the next two sets of four lanes to get to the petrol station, now clearly visible through the trees. And, of course, we will have to repeat the whole process all over again to get back to the car, assuming it will still be there.

But my fears are allayed. I discover, as we round the final curve of the huge roundabout, a footbridge over the next part of the eight-lane highway. I am less grateful when I see it is extremely rickety and in a very poor state of repair. It looks as if it might collapse into the road below at the slightest provocation. That doesn't bother Kevin, however. He bounds up the steps ahead of me, dragging me up and up until we reach the platform that leads over the road. Up there, the noise of the cars, lorries, vans, taxis and buses flying past below is deafening. The constant stream of vehicles in opposite directions gives me an instant shock of vertigo when I look down. I decide to fix my eyes on Kevin's waggling bum and the petrol station on the other side of the road, and try not to think about the metal torrent coursing past below me.

Finally down the other side of the footbridge, we stumble on to the petrol station forecourt like two castaways. It strikes me as rather odd to be in that sort of environment for the first time without the usual prerequisite of a vehicle in need of refuelling. I glance about and can't see any jerry cans. I panic initially, then realise they must be inside the kiosk. I have barely pushed open the door, however, before a shrill, harsh voice from behind a plastic screen at the other end shouts at me.

— No dogs in here.

— But I've...

— No dogs, the woman insists aggressively.

I look around at the smattering of other customers, who have all turned to stare at us.

— Look, I say, picking up Kevin, who licks his lips and contentedly settles into place. — I've run out of petrol on the roundabout up there.

I gesticulate with Kevin's body in the general direction of our car.

— I need to buy a jerry can and fill it up so I can go back and get my car out of danger. I couldn't leave my dog up there alone, I add.

I lift Kevin up like a prize lamb, as if to dispel any doubts over which dog I am talking about. The woman mulls this over for a moment.

— Okay, she says eventually, with an unmistakable air of resigned disappointment. — You can buy the can and fill it up, but don't put the dog on the floor, she hisses through clenched teeth.

I frown at her and wish to issue a pithy comeback, but decide I am in no position to argue, no matter how much her attitude irritates me.

— Where...?

— Over there, she barks, pointing to the far side of the shop.

I wander over to the spot indicated. I am increasingly hot and bothered with Kevin in my arms. I try to balance him while I struggle to pick up a jerry can. All the while Kevin gazes at me with an expression of amused disinterest.

— What about paying for the petrol? I ask when I get to the till.

The woman stares at Kevin with something approaching disgust.

— Go to that pump, she barks, nodding out of the window, — and fill it up. You can leave the can outside while you come back in and pay.

Back on the forecourt, I decide to ignore the woman's attitude and instead focus on trying not to spill petrol all over myself or Kevin. Putting a highly flammable liquid into the rather light and flimsy plastic can, while bent down almost to the floor and holding on to a dog lead, turns out to be quite a fiddly task. I hope Kevin doesn't take a sudden shine to anything, such as a passing squirrel, and bolt off, knocking over the can in the process.

Once I have gone back in and paid, we head to the car. The petrol sloshes about urgently in the jerry can as we walk.

— I said I needed to take you for a walk today before we went to see our friends, but I never imagined it would be like this.

We are recrossing the rickety bridge as I say that. Doubtless Kevin cannot hear me over the roar of the traffic. In any case, he has his head low and level with his back and his ears down, a pose he adopts when he is desperate to get out of a situation, but realises that complaints would be futile.

Back at the eight lanes of traffic, I decide, perhaps foolishly, to carry both Kevin and the jerry can. I bide my time, hoping not to trip over the central reservation. I observe now, as we wait for the optimum moment, that the traffic onto and off the roundabout is more rhythmical than constant. This makes our passage much easier and more comfortable the second time around, as I am aware I don't have to run for our lives once there is a break in the stream of vehicles.

Finally over on the other side, I pop Kevin onto the front seat of the car and empty the contents of the jerry can into the tank. I feel a huge sense of relief when I close the petrol cap and screw the lid back onto the can. I break out into a smile and decide that, one day, I will laugh about the whole story.

I put the can into the boot, wondering if I will ever use it again. Congratulating myself on a job well done, I rehearse in my mind starting the car and kicking it into gear, before rolling it into the four lanes of traffic.

Then a police car, sirens wailing and lights blazing, hurtles towards us at speed. It mounts the grassy bank inches from the car, just missing us. Then it pulls up in front of us in a slide that wouldn't have been out of place in a rally.

CHAPTER 20

⸎

I glance nervously at Kevin as I walk around the car to the rapidly advancing officers. They got out of their patrol vehicle at the kind of speed I imagine is normally reserved for tackling an armed robbery. Kevin looks back at me with what I presume is the same 'What now?' expression I have on my face. My fear is they will arrest me. I immediately panic for myself, but more for Kevin. What will happen to him if they take me away?

— I... I ran out of petrol, I stammer. — Coming down the M11. I couldn't find anywhere to fill up. I went there to get some, I add, gesturing towards the other side of the roundabout and the swaying treetops.

— Yes, we saw you on CCTV, one of them says, while the other checks out my car. — Are you all right?

— Now, yes. I am.

I follow the other police officer with my eyes before turning back to the first one.

— I had to have some help getting up onto the bank. Once the engine cut out, the momentum wouldn't get me far enough up. Two lads stopped and gave me a push.

— Oh yeah?

He is talking to me with the fake affability of a customs officer at a border desk. I have the distinct impression he has an ulterior motive. I think he is trying to catch me out. Or maybe that's just me feeling automatically guilty whenever I am around The Law.

— What did the two lads want?

— Oh, nothing, other than to help me. They literally stopped their car, got out, helped me push mine onto the bank, then left. They were really nice.

The first policeman pauses his interrogation to let his colleague finish his rounds. Then they both stand in front of me, legs apart, leaning back, chests inflated by their stab-proof vests and all the kit on their bodies. They both wear a studied expression of seriousness that I presume they learned in police training college. They strike me as being like a comedy double act, and I half expect them to say: — 'Allo, 'allo, 'allo, what's all this then?

I look down at Kevin, who gazes back at me with a rather puzzled expression. I want to burst out laughing.

— We've had reports of someone pretending to have broken down and, when people stop to help them, robbing them and driving off. There's been two incidents in this area this afternoon.

— Oh, I say.

The two policemen stare at me seriously.

— Oh, you mean those lads? No, they were really nice, they wouldn't hurt a fly.

They continue to stare at me in the ensuing silence. The penny still hasn't dropped that they are trying to determine whether or not *I* am the robber they seek. And then it does, and my stomach flips.

— I think those lads drove a VW Golf or something of that nature. Anyway, I've been at the petrol station most of the time, so we wouldn't have been here even if the robbers had stopped.

I gesture to Kevin in the car and give him a smile. In my nervousness, I can't stop talking.

— And here's me thinking you were going to tell me off for putting the car here, I continue. — It was completely unintentional. The car just ran out of petrol over there, I add, waving my hand behind me. — I was lucky to make it here, to be honest. So stupid of me to think I could get all the way to the next petrol station.

One of the policemen shifts on his feet before speaking.

— It can't be helped, he says. — It's one of those things. I guess you'll be wanting to go on your way, then.

— Well, yes, that'd be great. Thank you.

— Just be on the lookout for anyone trying to flag you down. We've heard he's pretty dangerous. He's in a silver Mercedes.

— Okay.

I look down at my rather tired-looking racing green Vauxhall Astra hatchback and wonder how on earth they could think I could be anything to do with the robberies.

— Thank you, I add.

They turn away to get back into their patrol car. I am opening the door to my car when the two policemen swivel on their heels.

— Don't move, one of them barks.

— What?

I am stunned by their sudden change in attitude.

— Show us your insurance documents.

— I don't have them with me, I say, straightening up. I try to give Kevin a reassuring smile, even though I feel anything but assured.

— Why not?

— You don't have to have them with you. It's not a legal requirement.

— You must have something.
— Why?
— This car has been stolen.
— No, it hasn't.
— Prove it, show us your insurance documents.

I want to say mockingly that you cannot prove a negative, but I quickly realise all that would prove is my stupidity in trying to humiliate a police officer. Instead, I rack my brains.

— Oh, I have a scan of the documents on my phone. Hold on.

The policemen stare at me impatiently as I scroll through folder after folder on my phone. They look as if they may jump on me and cuff me at any moment.

— Ah, here we are.

The policeman in charge takes my phone and looks at the car again before reading the documents. After a moment, he hands back the phone.

— You can be on your way, he says briskly.
— Why?

He shifts on his feet and looks accusingly at his colleague.

— We typed the wrong number plate into the database.

I stare at them, dumbfounded.

— You can go on your way now.
— Thanks, I mumble.

I check the wheels of the car, relieved to see they are not buried in mud. I should have enough traction to get off the grass bank relatively easily.

— Oh, can you give me hand?
— What do you mean? asks the other policeman, who has hitherto been silent.
— Well, you're blocking the exit and I need you to give me the all-clear for me to reverse out into those four lanes of traffic.

MORE LIFE AS A DOG

I jerk my thumb over my shoulder.

— Oh, yeah, don't worry about that, we'll be on our way.

With that, they jump in their patrol car, slam the doors shut and accelerate at full speed off the grass bank and into the traffic, disappearing from sight in an instant.

I turn to Kevin, who still looks a mite worried, and sigh.

— How do we get into these scrapes?

He stares back at me expectantly.

— I guess we'd better be on our way, then.

He wags his tail, sits down on his haunches and gazes out the windscreen, ready for the off.

CHAPTER 21

After a slightly hair-raising plummet off the grassy bank and onto the roundabout, the rest of our journey to Walthamstow is easy; tranquil, even.

However, Kevin cannot seem to settle down as he had done before, with his head on the edge of the passenger seat and his nose in my way whenever I select second gear. Instead, he is up and alert, looking around, taking everything in. Perhaps our adventure on the roundabout made him feel he should be ready for anything. Perhaps he is right. In any case, he keeps looking over at me. I meet his gaze. He examines my face, maybe looking for clues as to how to react.

— It's all fine now, we're just going to see our friends. You like them, and they love you, so it's going to be a nice evening. I even brought your other bed with us, remember?

I look over to the back seat. He follows my eyes, licking his lips and dipping his head.

— So you'll be able to have a proper doze there, once you've had your dinner and played with everyone.

I wish, not for the first time, that we could actually converse together. I would love to hear his thoughts and feelings, especially after all we went through, and not be obliged to divine as much as I can from his eyes and his body language (and occasional growls and barks). He settles down, but I take a corner rather badly and he is back up on his feet, looking out of the window, making sure he misses nothing.

We manage to park near our friends' house. This is handy as I have not only to marshal Kevin, who is careering about like a maniac and bouncing off the end of his lead at every opportunity, but also his large ring-shaped bed, bag of selected toys, bottle of water, snacks and dinner, plus a gift for the hostess and my overnight bag, should we decide to stay over.

It is the first time we have visited their home. I feel strangely nervous as I press the bell. But my fears are allayed when they greet us heartily and beckon us in. They apologise for the petiteness of their house, then take our things, ask us about our trip and treat Kevin like a visiting foreign dignitary or member of the royal family.

Kevin clatters about investigating the place at full speed, sliding on the wooden floors at each change of direction. Our friends coo and fuss over him and announce to the others there that this is the long-awaited guest. Isn't he just as wonderful and adorable as they said? Don't they want to bundle him up and give him a big squeeze? Look at him running around; isn't he so beautiful and charming?

Trying to maintain this good impression of my canine companion, I attempt to stop Kevin sticking his nose in too many things, or knocking over too many ornaments. As I do so, I reflect that I have, not for the first time, slipped into being very much an afterthought at this social gathering. Apart from a cursory hello and a nod and a handshake from the other guests, I am largely ignored.

MORE LIFE AS A DOG

Is it frustrating? A little. Am I jealous? Really only a very little.

Ordinarily I detest being the centre of attention, to the extent it can bring me out in a cold sweat when it gets out of hand. And I detest entrances, as one is then forced to be the object of everyone's stares. At least at other times it is largely down to ourselves whether or not we are in the limelight. If we desire it, we can make a scene, either in the positive or negative sense. But to be forgotten and sidelined in favour of my dog?

It is not as if Kevin doesn't merit being fussed over, although he doesn't much like it either. But I admit I would occasionally like to be noticed a little more, even if it is simply to be given the opportunity to demonstrate my modesty. I have to acknowledge, however, that it is almost inevitable that Kevin would be the centre of attention. Not only because he is a lovely looking dachshund, but also because he offers up a fascinating paradox.

On the one hand, his undeniable charm and delicate beauty make him appear worried and vulnerable and in need of care. On the other hand, he has a fiercely independent streak and stubborn side to him that defy all attempts at control. It's a kind of a go-your-own-way attitude. This contrast becomes quickly apparent to anyone who spends any time with him, and it lies at the heart of his appeal. He is a fragile yet fearless loner.

Through that contradiction, combined with his almost total lack of body odour, Kevin seems able to unite both canine and feline tendencies, like a cat trapped inside a dog's body. That makes him strikes a chord in a certain kind of person, typically cat rather than dog lovers. They can become utterly obsessed with him, to the extent that they completely ignore me when I am in his presence.

All of which makes it all the more puzzling when

some people seem not to see him at all and, even when they do, remain remarkably indifferent. I could dismissively say they are not animal lovers and leave it at that. But that would be too easy.

I think about all of this as Kevin and I motor home at the end of the evening. I was offered a bed for the night, and Kevin's bed was offered a place on the floor next to mine. But I was emotionally and mentally pulled out of the evening by the reaction Kevin received when we arrived, and had trouble reconnecting. At times like these, I prefer simply to go back home and wake up away from everyone, with my steadfast companion by my side, licking my elbow to wake me up and force me out of bed.

As the miles tick away in the darkness, Kevin sleeps on the passenger seat beside me. I drive calmly, collectedly, so he can rest the whole way. Before we left London, I made sure I went to the nearest petrol station and filled up the tank. But that doesn't stop me checking the needle every few minutes, each time with a shudder as I remember what we went through that afternoon.

CHAPTER 22

A FEW MONTHS AFTER OUR INCIDENT AT THE roundabout, Kevin and I are ambling through the back streets of Camden on a lazy Sunday afternoon, on our way to meet friends at a local pub. I have not been there before and I have no idea what to expect.

What we find is a rather tiny place with trestle tables strung along the pavement. In its ambience, it occupies that strange, typically London space somewhere between a genteel country inn and an edgy city boozer. The clientele runs the gamut from borderline posh to bankers dressing down on a day off, to the kind of people who are drawn to Camden's semi-mythical reputation for nurturing alternative lifestyles, to what one might call the rougher element. A quick glance at the packed interior convinces us we should take the remaining free trestle table at the farthest end of the row, where the atmosphere is a little more sedate and there is no direct sunshine.

Kevin skips happily along the street as we pass the mass of loud and cheerful customers swarming the tables. I notice two rather large hard men in sunglasses trying to look inconspicuous on the other side of the road, but pay them no more attention. Once we are settled and Kevin has taken a drink from his water bowl, he clambers up beside me on to the wooden planks of the seats. He takes an age to find his place on the hard surface before finally lying down and laying his head on my lap, never really looking comfortable.

There are eight of us in our group and we take our time deciding on what we want to eat and drink. We then quickly fall to gossiping, having not seen each other in weeks. All the while, I gently stroke Kevin's ear and roll it between my finger and thumb. He contentedly licks his lips and occasionally swallows. This requires him to lift his head up awkwardly and lower it back down again. I do wonder whether he really wants to stay in that position, especially as his bum seems to be hanging off the wooden planks. But I decide he would rearrange himself, or at least let me know, if he wanted to move.

The two from our group who went to give the food and drinks order return from the bar in an excitable mood. We are mid-conversation, so don't pay them much attention, but when they sit down and huddle close to us, they butt in.

— You'll never guess who's here?

We immediately stop talking and stare at them, slightly resentful at the interruption.

— Who? someone asks.

— Go on, guess.

— I can't, just say.

They both draw in their breath, look at each other with a conspiratorial smirk and whisper hoarsely: — Amy Winehouse!

One of our number goes to turn around.

— Don't look!

— But where is she?

— Over there, one of them says, motioning down the row of trestle tables. — Sitting at a table.

— Is she on her own?

— I don't know, the other one says. — She's talking to someone, but I'm not sure if she knows them. Those must be her security people, she adds, motioning to the two heavies across the street.

I turn around. One is watching something on his mobile telephone while the other stares into space.

— If they're looking after Amy Winehouse, they aren't paying her much attention, I murmur, still stroking Kevin's ear.

After a few more whispered comments, we go back to our prior conversations, and don't really think much more about Amy Winehouse. After all, no one else is paying her any attention.

Once the food arrives, all thoughts of other people, let alone world-famous musicians, are banished from our minds. Kevin had been semi-dozing with his head on my lap, but multiple roast dinners landing on the table at the same time cannot be ignored.

He sniffs the air with a ferocity that makes me think he would try to grab something, or at least beg with doe-eyes and a pitifully sad expression for a morsel from one of our plates. In the end, he looks, he cranes his neck, he sniffs again and again, then settles back down. Either he isn't hungry, or he is having one of those rare days when all my years of lessons, instructions and admonishments have sunk in. Whatever the reason, he is docile and perfectly still.

With everyone having received their order, we throw ourselves into our Sunday lunches with abandon. The drinks flow at a steady rate, and we settle into our usual risqué tipsy chat, shifting fluidly from one topic to another. This afternoon, and the lazy, hazy sunshine bathing everything in a golden glow, could last forever. Then one of our number stops mid-sentence and pops her head up like a meerkat. She raises an eyebrow and smiles.

— What is it? someone demands.

— She's coming over.

— Who?

— Amy Winehouse, she answers in an impatient tone. — She's going down the tables, talking to everyone in turn.

— Oh? What is she talking about?

— I don't know, I can't hear, but she looks drunk, she adds in a sympathetic tone that suggests the adjective 'very' or 'extremely' wouldn't have been wide of the mark.

We carry on talking, but we can hear Amy's famous Estuary drawl in the background, getting closer and closer. We realise she is at the next table, so maintain an increasingly faux and stagey conversation while we prepare ourselves to accept whatever happens next as if it is utterly normal.

I have my back to her, but eventually I see her out of the corner of my eye. Kevin had gone back to semi-dozing once we started eating, but Amy's arrival changes everything. He immediately stands up on his front paws and stares at her quizzically.

— All right? she asks when she reaches our table. — How's it going? Are you all having a good time?

We are, we tell her. Is she having a good time?

— Yeah, yeah. What are you guys up to today?

— Just having Sunday lunch together, the woman who spotted her arrival replies happily. — It's nice to be able to catch up.

— Yeah, that's great. It's so good to spend time together. It's really important.

She looks around at each of us in turn. I catch her eye. She is far more than drunk. She is so intoxicated, she can barely focus. Her face is passive, empty. Her long, loose movements suggest she could fall to the floor at any moment. And she is thin, painfully thin. I shudder to think how far she is from the bright, striking, radiant young woman I had seen bubbling with life in interviews and on stage just a few months ago.

She glances at Kevin. I want her to notice him and like him, and remark on his loveliness. I would like to introduce them. But she scans past him without even a flicker, and—oddly, stupidly, childishly—I am frustrated with her.

You, of all people should be able to truly see him; you who see so much in this world.

— You know what? she asks.

She grabs a small saucer of olive oil that was brought out with balsamic vinegar to accompany chunks of delicious locally made bread while we waited for our lunches to arrive.

— You should use this.

She opens her hand to reveal the most remarkably decorated and impossibly long fake fingernails, and scoops one into the olive oil like a camogie player hooking a ball. Once her nail is full of olive oil, she lifts it up and brings it to her other outstretched forearm. We all watch her in utter amazed silence. Kevin, on the other hand, is evidently uninterested in this person who is uninterested in him, and puts his chin back on my lap. Amy then tips her fingernail and wipes the olive oil up her forearm, before rubbing it in to her skin with her fingertips.

— See, it goes on like that, she says. — And you get this amazing suntan after, like you're frying in olive oil.

She gives a big laugh and looks around at us all, smiling but vacant. We laugh in return.

— You should try it, she says. — It's really nice on your skin.

None of us knows what to say, other than to

murmur noises of appreciation and thanks for her advice.

— It was really nice to meet you all, Amy says after a moment.

Again, she gazes at each of our faces in turn. She was once so beautiful, I reflect, and to see her reduced in this way makes my heart lurch with pain for her. I am also angry with her, not because she didn't notice or care for Kevin, but because she is destroying herself.

And yet, even in her extremity of excess and intoxication, swaying in front of us as if she is on her last legs, she still wants to connect, to converse. She wants to pass on her advice and to care, and show the light that shines within her, even if she is doing all she can to put it out.

She leaves us and ambles to another table. After discussing her without much enthusiasm for a moment or two, and agreeing on how sad and how much of a waste it all seems, we go back to our previous conversations.

By the time we leave, I am a little tipsy. I forget for a moment that Amy is at the pub and talked to us. But, as Kevin leaps down from the bench and pootles along the road, unusually subdued and calm after resting for so long, I note the bodyguards are still lounging about across the road, checking their phones.

We walk the length of the trestle tables. There, about halfway along, is a young couple having Sunday lunch together. The woman has her back to me, but I see an awkward expression on the man's face as he talks to his partner. He is a big man, with a huge chest and massive shoulders. I notice, propped gently against his left arm like a peaceful parrot, is Amy Winehouse, asleep, calm, in her own world.

It is a ridiculous scene. I might have laughed, especially as, when I was a teenager, I once fell asleep on the shoulder of a similarly proportioned man on a train, and he kindly didn't wake me up, or move, until I woke up myself in time for my stop.

But the underlying sadness of the situation stops me. I glance across at the bodyguards. I want to go over and remonstrate with them for letting her, a hugely talented and world-famous star, get into this situation. But maybe they would tell me she is a grown woman, that they are there only to protect her and that, right now, she is doing fine. Not knowing what to do or think, I put her out of my mind and focus instead on Kevin skipping along the road while he idly looks for scraps of discarded food to scavenge.

A few short months later, Amy Winehouse died.

PART III
THERE IS NO GREATER LOVE

CHAPTER 23

When I first got to know Kevin, and he me, we lived in London near Regent's Canal, in the less salubrious neighbourhood part-way up Caledonian Road. This was before the whole area around the canal was remodelled and turned into a strange mix between a theme park romanticising the area's dark industrial past and a wonky attempt to be 'modern'.

It would be tempting to say it was better in the old days, before all of the developments, but that would be a lie. It was, back then, a rough, crime-ridden area. The maze-like estates and low-rise death-trap towers reminded me of the wind-swept, urine-stained blocks I knew when I lived in Leicester in my youth.

The area around Caledonian Road was awash with marginalised people, who were largely ignored and constrained in an inescapable poverty trap that tipped many into drug addiction, prostitution or both. It felt a million miles away from the glossy, rich areas of the capital, just a few miles away.

But it was a 'real' area, in that it had trundled along organically for centuries, having some ups and plenty of downs. The people who lived there were there for a reason: because they were born in the neighbourhood and had nowhere else to go, or because they ended up there by chance and found they had nowhere else to go. Either way, they were, whether they liked it or not, invested in the community.

We chose to live there, in a flat above a shop on Caledonian Road, because the rental costs for somewhere within walking distance of King's Cross station and central London were so ludicrously low, I could, for the first time in my life, contemplate saving up a deposit to buy a home of my own. However, I quickly discovered why the area was so cheap when I heard gun shots almost as frequently as I had done when living near an estate of a very different kind in the countryside.

One morning, as I was leaving the flat with Kevin, a security guard taking money from the Iceland frozen food supermarket, not more than 100 yards away, was shot in the leg by teenage wannabe gangsters. We were coming out of the back garden when we heard it. I saw the kids run past with their bag of swag towards the park where I was intending taking Kevin for a walk.

The police later told me that the bag couldn't be opened without special equipment, and in any case didn't contain any money, so they had shot the poor man for nothing. The perpetrators were not caught, however, as anyone with knowledge of the estates, and who knew a friendly face living there, could disappear completely within moments.

That episode encouraged me to take Kevin the other way for his walks: not further into the estates as we had done every single time we went out, but across Caledonian Road and up the side streets towards Islington. On that fateful morning, I discovered not that the riches and glamour of London were a few miles away, but that they were just a few yards away, on the other side of the tired and pock-marked buildings that faced us every time we looked out the window.

This discovery of a whole new world right on our doorstep led to a huge evolution in our relationship, as together we explored and fell in love with the warren of charming streets that seemed always to lead us somewhere new and fascinating.

And we no longer had to deal as much with the simmering resentment, suspicion and anger that lay just under the surface in the people around Caledonian Road. Consequently, our daily walks went from being a chore to being a pleasure. I don't think we ever went the old way again, except for the briefest of walks when Kevin needed a wee late at night, or when it was raining and neither of us wanted to be out for long.

CHAPTER 24

THE NADIR OF OUR TIME LIVING AROUND CALEDONIAN Road came while I was driving back from a weekend away in a hire car.

Rolling down the hill from Pentonville Prison in the usual slow-moving train of vehicles on a Sunday afternoon, I chattered away while Kevin sat in the back. He paid me the smallest degree of attention, being doubtless all my banal conversation merited. I was happy—cheerful, even—as I took in the people milling about on the streets. It was a balmy day and all seemed right with the world.

As we reached the rather insalubrious Doyles Tavern, a man with a blond mullet, matching denim jeans and jacket and a wild look on his face ran out of the pub. He looked neither to the left nor to the right and dashed straight across the road between the cars, passing inches in front of us, before disappearing. A few seconds later, another man, thicker set, with short dark hair and an angry, determined expression, raced after him, also not looking before running straight onto the road.

As he reached our car, the dark-haired man raised his hand. I now saw he was holding a pistol. My heart leapt into my mouth and the breath stopped in my chest. He pulled the trigger. I was powerless to halt the car in time.

I saw the bullet whizz past the windscreen no more than an inch or two in front of us as we rolled along in ultra-slow motion. I tried to follow the bullet with my eyes, but to no avail. Time sped up again and the chasing man paused to let us pass before continuing his pursuit of his mulletted foe.

I don't remember anything else of the rest of the day, either before or after, but that moment burns in my mind as bright as a flash of gunpowder. I can still, even now, barely process the myriad might-have-beens, had we been just a few feet further down the road when he fired, or rolling slightly faster than at a snail's pace.

I suppose it was inevitable that, when the seething undercurrent of trouble in the area did finally reach our lives, it should have been triggered by Kevin, who was as capable of mindless violence as the next dog, if the circumstances led that way.

It was early on in our time together. I was not yet aware of how volatile he could be, or what could set it off. I knew, having experienced it many times, how jumpy he could be at home.

Every time the doorbell rang, he would have a panic attack and become uncontrollable for a few very fraught months. He would scrabble like a mad thing to get to the door and presumably do untold harm to whoever was on the other side, all the while wailing and howling at the top of his voice as if he had been badly hurt.

I wondered if he might be thinking his old family had come to take him back into what must have been a horrible period of his life, judging by the anxiety and depressive symptoms he regularly displayed during our early years together. That he was scared of going back to them was also obvious from his evident hatred, and fear, of stocky, squat white men with shaved heads and bull necks. This was the profile of his former owner to a tee. Kevin would either go for such men in a blind rage, or run away from them in an equally blind panic, but either way, he never missed an opportunity to bark at them.

The contrast with how he acted around women and people from ethnic minorities, to whom he seemed instinctively drawn, was quite remarkable. As the years passed and we eventually moved away from Caledonian Road, so saw fewer squat white men with bull necks, these extremities of response eventually evened out, and he merely judged people in the same way as most dogs: on the quality of their soul.

But in those early days, I was still learning about his predilections, his fears and what triggered them. It was easy to forget he could turn from being a cute, happy-go-lucky dog to a snarling, snapping menace in an instant.

ONE SATURDAY MORNING, we are walking down Regent's Canal towards Kings Cross. This is long before the towpath would be redeveloped, and the area is so derelict it seems as if one is trespassing in a place London would rather forget.

Kevin is pottering along in the grass verge, minding his own business, checking out the dandelions and daisies. In between sticking his snout into the flower heads, he sniffs and snorts at, presumably, hints of dropped food treasures hidden in the grass, to be scavenged with relish.

I want to make progress; Kevin wants to tarry. Our final destination is Camden, a long walk away, and I urge Kevin to get moving. But I don't want to drag him when he is so obviously delighting in his morning perambulation. I didn't have much time with him during the week; I am still a few months away from going freelance, so am obliged to work in the office and come back at lunchtimes to take him out for a walk—hardly an ideal situation for either of us. So I walk on ahead, letting the lead out to its full length while Kevin explores behind me, and think nothing more of it.

As I approach a finely wrought iron bridge that catches my eye, I hear a shout, then a yelp that I know instantly is from Kevin. I turn in time to see a medium-height stocky white man with a shaved head and bull neck, stuffed into a very tight blue sports t-shirt and matching shorts, trying to kick Kevin. For his part, Kevin leaps back, yelping more in anger than in pain, as the man, who is clearly out for a Saturday morning run, seems not to have connected with him.

— What the fuck are you doing? I shout.

The man looks up with a furious scowl on his face and his mouth twisted in a snarl.

— Your dog bit me, he shouts back, with a hint of hurt surprise in his voice.

— Don't be ridiculous.

I am amazed to think anyone could accuse Kevin of doing something so inelegant as to bite them, especially on the leg as they run past.

— What the fuck is that, then?

The man turns his leg and I look down to see some blood on his ankle.

— Oh, come on, it's not that bad, there was no need to try and kick him.

I am angry at the man, but I realise that is a stupidly insensitive thing to say. I want to make amends, but it is too late for that. The man is red with rage and, with all his force, swings his fist at my head and hits me as hard as he can on the left cheek.

Before I continue, I should remind you I am a black belt in karate. There are, to my mind, two gifts that such training gives you, the more important being the ability to stay calm and detached in stressful and violent situations. The other related benefit is the ability to set aside pain and not let it affect you. Consequently, his fist bounces harmlessly off the side of my face. While it hurts a little, I am able to completely ignore the fact that he just hit me.

— Look, I say, opening my hands and raising them in a supposedly calming gesture. — There's no need to...

But I see the man's face turn instantly from rage to bafflement to fear on seeing that his best shot has not, as he expected, put me on the floor and made me a cowering mess. On the contrary, it has had no effect on me whatsoever, to the extent that I didn't even acknowledge it. As he sees me raise my hands, his eyes widen in panic and he runs off as fast as his legs will carry him.

By now, Kevin is at my side. Realising it's too late to tell him off, as the moment has passed for him, I crouch down and check he is not injured.

— Are you okay? Not hurt anywhere?

Kevin jumps up and places his paws on my bent leg, then licks my face just below my lips, where my beard is beginning to regrow and the hairs rasp against his tongue. I give him a big hug and wonder what other ignominies and worries I will have to face as owner and companion of this sometimes troublesome hound.

CHAPTER 25

A LAZY SUMMER AFTERNOON IN A BACK GARDEN I DON'T know. Kevin and I have yet to move out of London, and we have been invited to a friend of a friend's barbecue. Amazingly for England, the weather is glorious on a day we would like it to be. I have forgotten the host's name and I am standing a little away from the main action, drinking a beer and shooting the breeze with someone I have never met before.

The garden is rather long and narrow, and features a central run of grass with what one might generously call herbaceous borders on either side. Where we are standing is paved in the classic English suburban style of large concrete slabs cracked into several pieces and extremely uneven. I assume they must have been laid at least twenty years previously and left to fend for themselves.

To top off the clichéd London garden chic, the herbaceous borders largely consist of weeds interspersed with the odd defiant hardy annual. They were clearly planted several years ago by previous tenants and are now refusing to give up, no matter what nature and the city can throw at them. The lawn also has large patches of bare, worn-out earth. I imagine how nice it could all look with a little TLC, especially as I can see there are more dandelions and thistles among the scarce blades of grass than anything else.

The space reminds me so much of my youth in the suburbs of Leicester that I have a flood of memories of all the hours I spent in our very similar back garden, trying to hem in the wanderlust I had learned while living in the open countryside. There, I had been used to going out the back gate and heading into a wood or field and being utterly alone and unseen. I had been able to roam wherever I wanted, with no real limits, and I revelled in a sense of freedom I took for granted and thought was available everywhere.

I was later forced to accept that it was a rare privilege, and standing in that rectangular suburban patch of threadbare London greenery, I experience again the intense, crushing sense in our Leicester back garden of being boxed in and observed by the neighbours in the surrounding houses, who I imagined were perpetually staring at me from the upstairs windows.

As I watch Kevin potter about, I understand that many of my frustrations and sense of claustrophobia came from this change in circumstances during my childhood. Once I was old enough, I would wander far and wide in Leicester, trying to find solitude and a place where I could simply 'be'; where my mind could wander where it would, without thinking of anyone or anything else, other than the flowers and insects, and the occasional animal.

I never found it.

Not that any of this bothers Kevin. I am only half concentrating on the conversation, and even on the barbecue in general, as I am fascinated by what my canine companion is up to. He is in his element, exploring every last inch of ground, sniffing every blade of grass and sticking his long nose into every flower and plant. I wonder if he can smell cats, or if it's the smell of grilled meat swaying down the breeze, but he has the air of a dog possessed, leaving no stone unturned in a quest for something he probably could not define, even if he were capable of doing so.

Now, in this garden, he is a furry missile, locked on to every target that takes his fleeting fancy, and judging by his sudden changes of direction, frequent snorts and obsessional sniffing, his fancy is taken by something new roughly every four seconds.

What makes the scene all the more fascinating is that he is being pursued by two boys aged no more than two or three years, who in their red-faced joy are following Kevin's every twist and turn with impressive dedication. Everywhere he goes, they are a few centimetres behind, laughing excitedly, arms outstretched, desperate to grab him and presumably give him a hug.

Kevin seems utterly oblivious to the pandemonium going on behind him, as he heads from flower to bush to patch of grass and back again. I know he has extremely keen hearing and is very aware of everything around him, so I am left with the impression that he is studiously avoiding the two boys, making sure he is always one step ahead and out of reach of their tiny, podgy, grabbing fingers.

At some point, I must have given a sharp intake of breath, as Kevin instantaneously slips out of the way of his pursuers and heads over to me to check that everything is okay. The boys bang into each other and almost fall over, like Keystone Cops. I ask the host, who I have barely spoken to, if they are okay.

— Don't worry, they love chasing him around. He seems like a very nice dog.

— Oh yes. He's lovely with kids, although he does sometimes try to avoid them.

We watch Kevin go back to his endless searching, sniffing and snorting, and the boys resume their chase.

— He's very patient with children, I continue. — I was just worried one of the boys will hurt themselves.

— It'll do them good to realise he's not a toy and has a mind of his own.

We talk on. I drink a few more beers and revel in the hazy alcohol fizz meandering through my veins and mixing with the afternoon heat of the late summer sun.

Eventually, we eat, and Kevin comes back to check out what's what. I give him his dinner and a bowl of water, then he resumes his exploration of the garden. Everything seems just perfect.

The afternoon turns into evening and those of us still there sit down and have a few more beers, talking through well-rehearsed London nonsense conversations. We enjoy that rarest of things: a moment of pure simplicity drawn out of the tumbling kaleidoscope of daily life in the capital, even if it is just for an afternoon and evening. It is almost as if we are on holiday.

CHAPTER 26

As evening turns into night, I recall our long journey home on public transport and decide it is time for Kevin and me to leave.

I call out his name.

Nothing.

I call again.

Nothing.

— That's strange.

— Anything wrong? my host asks as he passes.

— Kevin always comes, or at least responds, when I call him.

— Maybe he's down the bottom of the garden.

— If he is, he's been down there a long time. Are you sure there's no way out?

— I'm sure. There's a shed at the end. I suppose he could have got behind it, but it's all fenced off.

— With his shape and size, he can fit through the most unlikely gaps, I say.

I stand up and march down the garden. By now, my heart is in my mouth and I'm afraid to think the worst.

I call again.

Nothing.

I reach the shed. There are holes in the fencing.

They're filled with enough undergrowth to prevent a person from going through, but not Kevin. My heart sinks and I wonder what on earth could have happened.

I call again, more urgently this time.

Still nothing.

Then, what sounds like half a mile and several gardens away, I hear Kevin barking. A Jack Russell barks in response. Fearful Kevin could be in a fight and I have no way to reach him or save him, I shout his name as loud as I can. I sense the people from the barbecue are gathering behind me. I turn around to see several worried faces in the falling light.

— That was his barking, I say. — God knows where he is.

— How will you get him back? someone asks. — How will you find him?

I turn and shout his name again.

— Kevin! Come back here!

It dawns on me he will never return if he thinks I will tell him off. He has always had an issue with returning to me when I am angry. Now desperate, I rack my brain and wonder what on earth I can do to get him to make his way back over to this garden, if he even knows how to get there. For my part, I have no idea how far away he is, let alone where he is. Any search would be almost futile, and going from garden to garden would be out of the question, especially in the dark.

I remember the time he slipped his lead when my ex-wife and I had only had him for a few weeks. I tried to call him back, but he wouldn't come. Then, I recalled that he loved, at the time, playing with my keys. So I threw them on the ground in front of him, and he came immediately over and let me place the lead back around his neck.

That's it!

— Kevin! I shout at the top of my voice — Do you want a treat?

I take his bag of treats out of my pocket and shake them.

— Here you are, Kevin. Here's your treats. Do you want one?

It must be only a few minutes, but it feels like an eternity as I wait, then call out to him, then wait, then call again into the dark silence of the encroaching night.

Even if he hears me and decides to come back, will he be able to find his way?

It occurs to me that he went wherever he is without thinking at all, let alone with any idea of returning. And we all know how routes we have taken in one direction look utterly different on the way back, especially at night. The idea I will ever see him again seems impossible, ludicrous even, and tears come to my eyes as my heart breaks a little.

And then, when everything seems lost and I am bracing myself to turn and face the people waiting anxiously behind me, he appears. He pokes his head through a gap in the fence that he cannot get through. He is shaken, dishevelled, scratched and scared, but he is back. I am so happy and relieved, it is utterly overwhelming.

— Oh, Kevin. So you *do* want a treat, I say, laughing.

He wags his tail so hard his head shakes, but he panics when he finds he can't fight his way through the gap. Realising he must have left the garden via a larger hole, I search along the fence, finally finding one tucked behind the shed, now barely visible in the dark. I have to point it out to him several times before he calms down enough to understand what I mean. Once he does, he pulls his head back out of the smaller hole, scrambles through the undergrowth and drags himself through the larger one.

Once he is back in the garden, he runs over to me. I kneel down and he jumps up into my arms and licks my face all over. Behind me, I can hear the sighs and happiness in everyone's voices, and even a smattering of applause.

CHAPTER 27

I AM DISTRACTED, WANDERING THE STREETS WITH NO purpose, unsure where to go. I cannot work. I cannot even sit still. I simply have to keep moving. I don't have any choice.

It's a lovely day. Everything is in bloom, people included, after several weeks of inclement weather, but I can't really take it all in. How can I? I am too distraught, too worried. And what's making it worse is I am having to pace the streets alone. The only thing that could make me feel calmer and help me deal with everything in a rational, reasonable manner is the object of my concerns.

A FEW WEEKS AGO, I noticed Kevin was not eating properly. He didn't lose a lot of weight, but he did slim down noticeably. At his age, that is hardly a sign of being on top form. But I hoped he would rediscover his appetite as a matter of course. And, like all worried parents, carers and pet owners who are deeply attached to their charges and fret over their welfare constantly, I tried to ignore it and hoped it would go away.

It didn't.

Then one day, I noticed him wincing while he ate. I barely saw it, just as my head was turning away after I put down his bowl. I stopped and watched him properly this time. There it was again: an unmistakable wince on the left side as he ate his kibbles. He tried to assuage the pain by taking a drink of cold water before eating, but it clearly had little effect.

My heart sank, partly as it is always very difficult seeing him in pain and partly as he's had numerous cleaning treatments in recent years to remove thick layers of plaque. This always made me feel I am a Bad Owner. I guessed this wincing was a clear escalation that would entail lengthy and involved treatment, and would cause him a lot of discomfort.

Another, rather selfish, reason my heart sank is that, on top of the inevitable impact of all the resultant appointments on my work, the treatment could cost me a small fortune. Experience has taught me that pet insurance is useful only for the first treatment your loved one has for a new condition. Once they have undergone an intervention or received medications, all subsequent management for that and related conditions will be struck from the insurance coverage. Consequently, future costs will have to be paid out of pocket. And the fees for even the most basic procedures can be astronomical.

However, it was obvious I couldn't ignore the problem, not when he suffered every time he ate.

So we found ourselves in the consulting room, Kevin standing on the table with a perturbed expression on his face after a rather uncomfortable examination of his mouth and, for good measure, the rest of him. After being given a detailed description of what my beloved companion had wrong with him, I was told —and this was the worst part—that all of his dentinal travails were my fault. Unwittingly, of course, but my fault nonetheless.

I HAVE GIVEN KEVIN, from a young age, what I call chewy sticks, meaning long, straight treats moulded into a sort-of star shape. They are sold as being good for dental hygiene, the theory being they scrape between his teeth while he enjoys a tasty snack. That he has become somewhat obsessed with them is clear by the anger and frustration he shows every time they aren't available, particularly when we are at home and they have run out. It is as if the outrage of me forgetting to buy more and ensure adequate supplies is far worse than merely not taking some with us when we go out.

Now, over a decade later, I found myself being chastised by a well-meaning but clearly irritated vet, who has had to explain to yet another unwitting dog owner that those chewy sticks are actually highly addictive to dogs and contain all sorts of awful ingredients.

This stung, as I spent a lot of time and effort researching the ideal diet for a canine of his breed and size. Initially, this was to prevent his urinary incontinence, but I also wanted to give him a regime that would keep him in the best of health, all the while respecting the environment and ensuring the carbon footprint of his food would be as small as possible.

I found a special mix that, frankly, transformed his health, and I have always been proud that he seems in such great shape. He looks physically fit and has a glowing coat. And yet, here was a vet, an expert in dog health, telling me I had overlooked a key poisonous detail. It was as if I had given someone very dear to me the best of everything, reduced their meat intake and cut out all unhealthy and processed foods, only to let them carry on smoking.

And then came the bombshell: not only are those chewy sticks, to which I have let my dog become addicted and allowed him to eat for years and years, bad for his health, but they have ruined his teeth. It turns out they are incapable of even the one task they set themselves: 'cleaning' his teeth and gums by pushing away food and other detritus through the mere act of chewing.

I was appalled. I stared down at Kevin, still standing on the examination table, with apologetic horror. For his part, he had got over his discomfort and was gazing back at me with an expression of benign comfort. It only made me feel worse.

— So, I have created this problem, by giving him those chewy sticks?

— I'm sorry, but their teeth end up with a sugary, sticky coating. This causes plaque to form and damages their gums.

I stared at the vet.

— So, what's next? What does he need?

— It looks like I'll have to take out two teeth here, he said, pulling Kevin's upper lip back and gesturing at the left side of his mouth. — And I'll do a deep clean of the rest, with the hope that I can stop them from rotting like these.

I shuddered when I glanced down at Kevin's happy face.

— Will he need a general anaesthetic?

— Yes. Taking out a tooth is a major procedure. He needs to be unconscious for the deep clean anyway.

I imagined Kevin lying on the operating table, out cold, his tongue lolling like a slice of ham, a dead expression in his eyes and a tube coming out of his mouth. I didn't go as far as imagining him being operated on, but saw him more as an animal in a laboratory. I shuddered again. I wished Kevin wouldn't keep looking at me in that trusting, heartfelt manner.

I am a Bad Owner.

— How much will it cost? I asked without looking at the vet.

I didn't really listen to the answer. Of course, I mentally checked he didn't say it would cost a million pounds, but I didn't take in the actual numbers. I asked the cost because I had to, because it would be negligent not to, but all the while knowing the specific figure wasn't going to change anything: Kevin needed his operation, I would pay for it and that was that. The 'how' was immaterial. That the procedure would be performed was the only important thing. That and Kevin recovering enough to be able to eat normally and forget all about this terrible episode.

But he would end up with two teeth missing, and the vet didn't talk about what he would do to rectify that, other than to say that it wouldn't affect Kevin too much and he would get used to it. I knew that already. He, like all animals, is remarkably adaptable. He has got used to everything life can throw at him, once he gets over the initial pain or discomfort and starts to feel better.

The only question left to ask was when the operation would take place. The vet told me in just two days. So, we left, me with my heart on the floor and Kevin bouncing down the street, happy once again to have visited one of his favourite places. This is doubtless because he is fussed over and made the undeniable centre of attention. It was a shame, I reflected, that after the next visit to the vet, he might never be so well disposed towards the place again.

CHAPTER 28

I DECIDE TO TAKE ADVANTAGE OF A LOVELY AFTERNOON to extend our walk into the countryside. This time, we eschew the charms of Burghley Park and head instead onto the meadows. We follow the river out of town and towards the bright yellow fields of oilseed rape beyond.

I enjoy the walk, but any enjoyment is tainted by knowing Kevin has, thanks to my inattentiveness over his snacks and treats, arrived at a point where his teeth are so bad, he needs two of them removing. I think back to him wincing while trying to eat, and the pang of guilt feels like a dull blade pushed into my side. I hate to see him suffering. I feel his pain as if the wound is my own.

The only thing for it is to let him have the operation.

The following couple of days are difficult for me, although less so for Kevin. The vet has given me some painkillers and they have eased the pain somewhat when he eats, although he still looks uncomfortable.

I am not happy he has to go under general anaesthetic, and wish, like an anxious parent, I could go through it in his place, so he doesn't have to suffer. But I can't, and he doesn't know what is about to happen.

So there is no point in dwelling on it too much, especially as all I can do now is wait.

When the day finally comes around, we head over early in the morning to the unprepossessing, utilitarian low red-brick building that serves as the veterinarian's surgery. Kevin skips happily along the street, all the more so when he realises we are not going into town, but rather back to his favourite place.

In the waiting room, I am nervous and resigned. He stands on the floor, upright and proud. His head is up and his tail is straight and quivering with a slight wag that never fully forms. He stares at the door to the consulting rooms, anticipating us being called in and him running up the ramp. He occasionally glances at me as if to ask why we haven't been called, then looks back to the door.

— It could be a while, Kevin. You may as well relax and wait. Do you want to sit on me and have a rest?

I pat my thighs. He looks at me, then down at my legs, then returns to staring intensely at the door. Clearly he does not want any rest, but rather wants to get into the consulting room as quickly as possible.

If only he knew what was coming, he wouldn't be so enthusiastic.

To distract myself, I inspect the racks of dog and cat toys and pet paraphernalia. They once again amuse me and bemuse me in equal measure. It never fails to amaze me how much rubber, plastic and fake animal fur is used up in creating the endless variety of objects sold as diversions for our apparently under-stimulated pets.

Don't get me wrong, I have enough dog toys and accessories to open a shop, but it strikes me that we have created a situation with our pets where we invest them with human-level expectations over their quality of life and how much they should be stimulated.

Only a generation or so ago, dogs and cats were functional accompaniments to our lives, and any pleasure we might have gained from their company was purely incidental. Now we fret over their wellbeing as if they were our children, and as if their development and the expression of their identity were a measure against which we, as owners, can and will be judged, often harshly.

I am no stranger to this. I believe in Kevin achieving as much self-awareness and fulfilment as possible. I would like to see his personality expressed to its maximum. I want his intelligence to be pushed, and him to communicate as deeply as possible. This is not because I am soppy or have some notion that he is a child replacement. Rather, I want to understand his capabilities and capacity for development.

Perhaps this is because, living in Leicester in the 1980s, I grew up in a community where being something more than the most ordinary and conventional person was both a betrayal and a pretentious statement that you believed you were somehow 'better' than those around you. That attitude held me back for a long time, and I now encourage anyone who wants to listen to be better and more fulfilled versions of themselves.

Beyond Kevin and the animals with whom we share our lives, how much could a wild animal express itself and communicate, if only we gave it the chance? Are we missing out on a connection and shared existence we have ignored for millennia simply to dominate and destroy the boundless life and variation that exists around us? Are we the ones eschewing what the natural world has to offer in our unidimensional view of it?

CHAPTER 29

I AM SNAPPED OUT OF MY REVERIE. THE CONSULTING room door has been flung open and Kevin's name is being called out in a clear, loud voice.

Kevin looks up at me, then runs to the ramp up to the consulting rooms, scrabbling on the floor with all his might when he reaches the end of his lead.

— He seems happy to be here, says the delighted veterinary nurse. — We don't get that very often.

But he won't be anymore, once today is over.

I follow Kevin into the coldly lit room and she closes the door behind us.

A FEW HOURS LATER, although it feels like days, I get a call. Yes, the operation went well, and yes, Kevin is fine. Two teeth were taken out, and he coped well with the anaesthetic.

When can I pick him up?

At the end of the day, around 6pm.

I put the phone down and a wave of relief rushes through me. I sit and my shoulders relax. Until that moment, when the nurse told me everything was okay,

I hadn't realised just how anxious and stressed I was about the whole thing.

A torrent of awful thoughts about how badly it might all have gone flood my mind. I must have been holding back like a dam. I try to ignore them. What is the use of thinking like that, especially now it's all over and there is nothing more to worry about?

I look around the flat. I haven't done anything since I got back earlier that morning. I've just wandered the house like a ghost, unable to sit down or really process anything. I was supposed to be working, but all that went out the window.

I stare at my computer. I should deal with my emails and the most urgent tasks. But I have no enthusiasm for work. I want to go to the clinic and sit in the waiting room until I can see Kevin. But that could be hours. He is in recovery, and will stay there a good long while. Not only does the general anaesthetic need to wear off, but also he has to show his bodily functions are normal before the vet will let him go.

The powerlessness of not being directly involved in any procedure and its consequences is one of the most difficult aspects of being a loved one, especially an owner or parent. I have gone under the surgeon's knife a few times myself. It is, at least for my personality type, far easier to be the patient, to know what is going on and deal with each thing as it occurs, than to be on the outside of the sterile white door, waiting endless, torturous hours, hearing nothing but the generic sounds of a vast healthcare machine that has taken your loved one into its inner workings and will only release them from its grasp when it is good and ready.

What can I do to while away the empty hours that lie before me, when the fear of the unknown has been only partly assuaged? I tidy, of course; my desk at first, and then more and more of my flat until it looks better than it has done in an age. I cook lunch, then clean, but without much enthusiasm and application. I look things up online that I am not interested in, then think about leaving the house.

After much procrastinating, I finally grab my coat and head up towards Burghley Park. I don't get far, however, before I think of how Kevin should be with me now. I want to walk somewhere, anywhere else. So, I explore the back streets and alleyways of Stamford, and head to places we have never been before. I distract myself and take a forced interest in passers-by and the buildings I come across.

But it does not take long before my mind returns to Kevin and the enduring image of him lying prostrate on the operating table, his eyes closed, his tongue lolling out and a tube coming from his mouth. I shiver and try to blame it on a gust of wind, although I know it's really because I can't bear the idea of him being in pain. It physically sickens me. I want more than anything for it to stop.

I wonder how I would react if he was my child and was ill.

I hope I'd be a little more together.

CHAPTER 30

IT OCCURS TO ME THAT PART OF THE PROBLEM IS I AM doing all this alone, and have been carrying Kevin's life by myself for nearly a decade.

Every little thing that goes wrong with him, everything he needs on a day-to-day basis, every time he needs to go to the toilet, every time we go for a walk or away on a trip, it is my responsibility to care for him and make sure every eventuality is covered. All day, all night, every day of every week, for years and years on end. I cannot do anything, cannot go anywhere, not even to the bathroom, without him being present and me having to think about him and his needs. He fills my every living second, and it weighs on me. I wish, not for the first time, I had someone in my life who would just say, even once in a while: — Don't worry, I'll take care of this. Leave it to me.

I have been in many relationships while Kevin and I have been together, and many women have wished to supplant him, or at least be his equal, in my affections. But no one who tried to worm their way between us has ever, not even once, wanted to share the responsibility of looking after him.

Am I picking the wrong people? Or is a dog one

person's responsibility, even when that person is in a relationship? Right now, today, waiting for Kevin to be released by the vet, I am single, and happy to be. But the way he completely dominates my mind and my heart is wearing me down. I would like to be able to step away, even for five minutes.

I think this with an increasing sense of guilt as I round, perhaps for the third time that day, the corner at the end of Stamford High Street. I look up and notice the clouds have blotted out the sun and darkness has filled the sky.

The phone rings. My heart jumps into my mouth.

I can come and pick Kevin up any time. He has woken up and is sufficiently recovered to go home. He will be a little groggy and not quite himself, but he should be back to normal by tomorrow.

Forgetting my earlier complaints, I am relieved and elated in equal measure. I smile at the clouds, at the passers-by, at anything and everything. I see other dogs walking along the street with other people and no longer feel the pang of absence, but the joy of knowing that will soon be us again, reunited, ready for new adventures and whatever life can throw at us. I imagine his bright, loving, trusting face gazing up at me as we walk happily along together, and us at the flat, playing or lying on the sofa as I watch a film or read a book.

By the time I get to the vet's, I am excited. The nurse asks me to wait a few minutes while the vet checks him one last time and gets him ready. I pay his bill, the final cost of which I try to ignore as I tap in my PIN. The nurse warns me Kevin will be tired and may not want to walk far. I brush off her concerns with a cheery smile. I tell her not to worry, I will make sure he is okay.

I hover by the counter for what feels like an eternity. After a few minutes, the nurse brings him out, bearing him aloft in her arms like a prince, and he brings all his noble bearing to the occasion. I grin from ear to ear and long for him to notice me. However, my face falls when he does. He gives me the dirtiest look he has ever given me and turns his head away haughtily, as if to say: — Don't you ever let them do that to me again.

Crestfallen, I go over to him. He won't look at me as the nurse explains what I need to do over the coming days to make sure he heals properly, what to feed him, and what to let him do and not do until he is ready to resume normal life. Kevin still won't look at me as she places him carefully on the floor, and I book a check-up appointment.

— He's been as good as gold, the nurse says. — He's such a lovely, gentle boy.

I recover myself, nod and smile.

— Thank you for everything, I say. — Shall we go, Kevin?

Still deliberately not looking in my direction or acknowledging my presence, he hesitates, then trots to the glass doors. He doesn't tug at his lead, presumably so he doesn't risk hurting himself, and waits patiently for me to open the door.

He walks down the road a few paces in front of me, staring straight ahead and choosing the shortest route back to the flat. He pretends for all the world that he is going for the walk on his own and I just happen to be sharing the pavement with me. It is fully two days before he will look at me directly, or make any indication of responding to what I say.

CHAPTER 31

Over the following weeks, Kevin's wounds recovered and he became better at eating, once the swelling had gone down and he got used to the gap in his teeth.

He even, after a while, tentatively started playing with his toys again, alone at first and then with me. Initially, he gripped them with his tiny front teeth, holding on gently but firmly, although he couldn't do it for long. Even though I tried to stop him, he ended up hurting himself more than once and bent one of his teeth. Then he tried gripping his assorted stuffed animals with the side of his mouth where the full complement of gnashers remained. Finally he started to seem more comfortable.

But it was undeniable that he had lost some of his enthusiasm for playing following the removal of those two teeth. They had been in the middle of the left-hand side of his mouth. In a certain sense, it made him unbalanced, and he was constantly aware of it.

Perhaps it was a coincidence, but he also seemed to age quite noticeably around the time of the operation. Much more grey fur came through, not just around his mouth. The formerly chestnut brown patches around his chops turned into something more like the week-old stubble of a middle-aged man. Then there was grey at his temples, followed by an even sprinkling of grey throughout his fur. The salt-and-pepper look suited him, however.

I also noticed he walked a little less quickly, and was less keen to dash about. Now he never ran to the end of his lead and hung there, scrabbling in desperation against the pavement to get to something. He merely waited for things to come to him.

Not that we stopped going on long walks. He could walk for miles and miles, trotting along at a steady pace, much closer by my feet than before. He often looked up at me now, seemingly to check I was still there, but perhaps also for reassurance.

He could still be driven wild by the smell of horses, and he would throw himself at flocks of pigeons and revel in scattering them. But he flung himself into such situations with less abandon and vigour, and the red mist passed much more quickly than before. Encountering another dog could also be a hit and miss affair, but he was much more likely to ignore them or offer up a stage-whisper growl under his breath, especially if the canine in question was on the other side of the road.

After a while, it occurred to me he had been ageing steadily for a good long time before the operation and had simply passed into another phase of his life. But his surgery had made me stop and observe that he was changing, or rather made me admit that we must inevitably adapt as we grow older and our lives evolve.

I had been aware that he had mellowed and matured after his early years, when he passed into adolescence, then young adulthood before he became a truly grown-up dog. Each time we had moved with the times, and now we must do so again. I couldn't, mustn't, expect that he would be the same animal, day-in day-out, forever. I had to acknowledge that he was now middle aged.

Actually, the truth I didn't want to accept was really not about Kevin at all. I hadn't wanted to face the fact that I too was getting older and heading into middle age. I myself needed to slow down, to reflect and use my experience to make better, wiser choices and to live well.

Watching Kevin go through that same process and us both learning to adjust our lives and expectations accordingly helped me to accept the change in myself. I initially used his venerable maturity as an excuse to say no to things, or at least do them in a way that suited us better. Then I started saying 'we' needed to do this or that, rather than saying it would be better for Kevin, before I could finally say 'I' wanted something.

Soon enough, we settled into a new rhythm, and moulded our relationship to the extent that, one day, I realised I was happier now than I had ever been. I had learned from Kevin's slower, more considered and wiser personality, and his new-found ability to use less energy to get what he wanted far more effectively than he ever had done before. I also finally forgave myself for the operation and the constant reminder from the gap in his teeth, although there was still the nagging sense of having let him down.

CHAPTER 32

Then the world turned once more and my life changed again. Or rather, I revisited a previous period of my life that I had, at the time, wanted to forget.

For a couple of years after my divorce, when Kevin and I were starting out on our journey alone together, I was asked to report from a few medical conferences. They had, for the most part, been in the USA, and it had been exhausting. Exhausting not because the job itself wore me out, although I worked harder in the few days I was in each city than I had ever done before in my life, but because I was not ready for travel, not like that.

Out on my own, out in the world? That was beyond me to handle in a mature and responsible manner, and it had been clear to me from the start. I managed to do the work itself, producing story after story after story to order, day after day. But it was the rest of the time that I found problematic. It didn't help that the colleagues who travelled with me wanted to do everything *sans limite*, drinking as long and as hard as possible each evening until they could drink no more, before getting up early the next day and starting all over again.

I fell in with that. I was easily led and somewhat immature in that respect. On the other hand, I see now with hindsight that I was struggling with the responsibility and demands of the job. I could handle it during the tumult of a news day at the conference, as there was hardly a second to think, especially if half of one's brain had been shut down due to a massive hangover. But it was in the cold and lonely hours afterwards when the fears, doubts and suspicions would creep in, like rats into a warehouse once all the workers had gone home and the lights had been turned off.

So I drank, nervously, guiltily at first, then with increasing abandon and self-hatred. I told myself I could handle it and, well, I would always get up the next day and get the job done. The drinking and the self-hatred spiralled until, at two conferences in relatively quick succession, the only real way of describing what happened was I tried to destroy myself through alcohol. I wanted to erase myself, to no longer have to be me.

Even at the time, I knew I was in trouble. I was already in therapy, but I was at a point where it seemed my head had been split open, and my entire life was being examined and rearranged. This was all under my own volition, of course, but at times I seemed no longer in control of myself. And as soon as a drop of alcohol passed my lips, I succumbed to an unnamed demon that possessed me, without my apparent knowledge or control.

Except that it was me all along, possessing myself, and I knew that, deep down.

Just as it reached a critical point and I almost lost touch with myself utterly, the travelling stopped. I was no longer called back to do a conference for that client. I naturally assumed it was because of my out-of-hours drunken escapades. I learned later it was simply because they had changed their focus and no longer wanted to send people halfway across the world to report on medical meetings.

So, I was back home, back with Kevin, having missed him terribly each time I was away.

A while later, I travelled again, maybe three or four times a year to conferences in Europe. This time, I was much better at my work and found it easier to handle. It had become apparent, again through therapy, that the unease had always been with myself.

And yet in the lonely hours of the dark, long nights, when everyone sensible had gone to bed, the emptiness within dragged me once more into awful self-reflection. So I drank and I drank until I was no longer able to contemplate the apparent nothingness of my life. I remember almost never going to bed on those trips.

It did not help that my client at the time seemed to be hell bent on manipulating those who worked for her, gaslighting them and failing to deliver on promises that, in hindsight, she could never have kept. Eventually, she ran out of money, and consequently so did I. It was then that I dipped down to my lowest point, until that fateful morning when Kevin placed his head in my hand and encouraged me to leave my bed and live once again in the world.

It took me years to achieve a level of personal stability, and to recover financially, after that period. I was happy not to travel for work for a while and instead focus on Kevin and myself. I learned to appreciate what we had, and what it gave us.

CHAPTER 33

By the time Kevin had his teeth removed and we had settled into a more stable, easy and comfortable life together, I had moved on entirely from that period. I no longer felt at the mercy of demons I could neither know nor control.

At that point, a new client, one with no connection with my past, asked me to report from a conference. I hesitated, as I wanted neither to leave Kevin nor to go back down that dark, hard path I had taken before. But I realised I would never know if I was capable of being sent to far-flung places on my own and holding it together, not just for work but also for myself, if I didn't try.

So with some trepidation, but also some excitement, I accepted. I felt immediately guilty, partly because I didn't want to be away from Kevin, partly because I didn't want to burden other people with looking after him.

That turned out to be the least of my worries, however. Now a venerable old gentleman, he made far fewer demands and needed fewer walks to burn off his energy than in his youth, and friends and family who might have hesitated over taking him for a few days were more than happy to welcome him into their home.

Perhaps we had all matured. Perhaps we had reached the stage when the white heat of youthful intensity had died down enough for us to step back a little and take stock. Perhaps that had allowed us to find, and offer, space in our lives for others and help those in need.

It assuaged my guilt over farming him out to others, although not entirely; even though these trips didn't occur very often, I would worry about him nonetheless. I saw, more and more as I took to the road once again, how delicate he is, and not only in older age after some knocks, but that he had always been.

Right from the beginning, he, like all dogs, probably all animals and certainly all people, was sensitive and liable to be hurt if mistreated. If he was pushed and pushed, that hurt could turn into a deep pain that would invert into a violent anger against anyone or anything that threatened him. It was his life's work, in a way, to reject that, and leave behind the pain he had suffered.

I could see that now, and that I had gone through the same journey myself.

I AM THINKING of all of this as I ride through London in a taxi. I have been away at another conference, for a few more days than I would have liked. But it went well. I am pleased with the work and what I achieved, and with how I approached the trip in general. For the first time, I am aware of being in control of myself, and of being content with my performance.

But most of all, I am happy. Happy to see the lights and the constant movement of London in the early evening, but especially so as I am about to be reunited with Kevin. I am impatient to see him. And excited. I want to be around him, to hold him, to feel his presence.

The taxi crawls along the streets of Shoreditch in the endless traffic, towards where friends have been looking after him. It only increases my sense of impatience and excitement. We round the last few corners on our way to the bar where I have been told to meet him and our friends. I am eager to get there.

I have never been to the bar before. It is in a small, intimate square I don't know. We turn the last corner and I see it is pedestrianised on three sides. The taxi stops in the far corner from the bar. From this vantage point, I can't see anyone, although I know Kevin must be there.

I close the door and drop my suitcase to the floor. I perform my little whistle I use to let him know I am around, or to call him back to me if he has wandered off.

Before I have even finished, I can hear the clatter of his paws on the cobblestones. I see him bound through the mess of chairs and tables like a slalom ski racer as he bolts towards me. I have not seen him run this fast in years. I can see the wild excitement not just in his eyes, but in his face and his entire body.

As he gets closer, I drop down on one knee, and open my arms wide.

— Hey, Kevin!

He runs the last few yards even faster. As he reaches me, he jumps. I grab him in my arms. He wriggles and wriggles as I hold him tight. He is desperate to lick my face, my chin, my ears, anything he can reach.

And I am at peace again.

ABOUT THE AUTHOR

L.A. Davenport is an Anglo-Irish author and journalist. He has been writing stories, and more, since he was a wee bairn, as his grandpa used to say. Among other things, he likes long walks, typewriters and big cups of tea.

To find out when L.A. Davenport has a new book out, and get the latest updates, visit his official website at Pushing the Wave.

PRAISE FOR L.A. DAVENPORT

[*The Nucleus of Reality* is] a beautifully described story of a man trying to remember why he ended up losing everything but himself.

— EMILY QUINN

[It] is strange, existential, and curious. It might give you a lot to ponder about if you dig deep enough…[It's] a stream of consciousness first-person novel with the most unreliable narrator you've ever met.

— RUMMY'S RECS

Trust me, you're in for a mind-bending ride…I had no idea how it would end.

— KAM BROOK

[*My Life is a Dog*] is a quick read, it's a sweet read, it's exactly the kind of thing to buoy your spirits after a long week (or 2020). I do recommend this for you or the dog lover in your life.

— THE IRRESPONSIBLE READER

There is only one word that could describe this book and that is adorable...I really adored this wee book and I adored Kevin and it's clear his owner also does! Such a sweet book.

— BOOKS BY BINDU

Readers [of *Escape*] will eagerly follow John's character arc from a self-destructive, grieving widower to an individual fighting to clear his name and take down a criminal organization.

— THE BOOKLIFE PRIZE

I wanted to know more, to see where the little strings led and ultimately see who was trying to *Escape*.

— PERRY WOLFECASTLE

If you're after a bit of a thriller combined with romantic suspense, then *Escape* is definitely one to add to your (probably ever growing) TBR list . . . I didn't want to put it down!

— EMILY QUINN

BY L.A. DAVENPORT

FICTION

The Nucleus of Reality, or the Recollections of Thomas P—
Escape
No Way Home
Dear Lucifer and Other Stories
The Marching Band Emporium

NON-FICTION

My Life as a Dog
More Life as a Dog

Printed in Great Britain
by Amazon